Teach Me To Play WITH You:

Easy Games, Songs, and Play Activities
to Teach Social Interaction
to Toddlers and Young Preschoolers
with Language Delays

Laura Mize, M.S., CCC-SLP

Pediatric Speech-Language Pathologist

teachmetotalk.com

P. O. Box 1231

Shelbyville, KY 40066

Contact: Laura@teachmetotalk.com

Cover by Brett E. Friedman at wyatt's torch web design.

The author and publisher are not responsible for injuries arising from the use or misuse of these materials and activities.

If your child is exhibiting any signs of speech-language delay, please know that he or she will be best served by being evaluated and treated by a licensed and certified speech-language pathologist.

Manufactured in the United States of America.

Dedication

This book is dedicated to my husband Johnny,
who makes me better than I could ever be on my own,
and who can take a sliver of a good idea and turn it into reality.
You are the reason teachmetotalk.com exists!

And

To our children Jonathan, Tyler, and Macy.

How can I be so lucky to have the four of you?

Acknowledgments

Thanks to all of the parents who have emailed me to ask for more ideas or specific directions after reading the post on my website, "Social Games for Babies and Toddlers." You are the inspiration for this project!

I want to thank the moms and dads of all the children I've personally worked with in and around Louisville, KY. Thanks for letting me learn from you and love your children! Many of these ideas were perfected in your homes.

Thanks so much to Kate Hensler, Developmental Interventionist, and my partner on "Teach Me To Talk with Laura and Kate," who read early copies of this manual and gave me invaluable feedback. Almost all of my projects are honed and polished during our many cell phone conversations between appointments, even if neither one of us realized it at the time. Your unwavering encouragement and support over these many years means more to me than you'll ever know. Thanks too for teaching me several of your own cute routines which are scattered throughout this book.

Thanks to my mother, Peggy Wright, for her eagle eye and assistance to edit this project and to my dad, Ervin Wright, for helping her. Most of all, thanks to the both of you for loving me and believing in me since the day I was born.

I would especially like to thank my husband, Johnny, for...well... everything!

Contents

Author's Note

I have spent most of the day putting in a comma
and the rest of the day taking it out. —
Oscar Wilde

I would like to take a moment to share that I am a practicing speech-language pathologist and not a professional writer. I did not consult one during this entire project because I wanted this material to reflect what I really do and say in my real-life, everyday work with young children, their families, and other therapists. Consequently, the information on these pages is written exactly like I would say it to you if I were meeting with you in person. Despite hours and hours of laboring to edit and re-edit this manual, I'm certain there are mistakes I did not find. In fact, there may be errors that I didn't know were wrong in the first place! For this I apologize, and most of all, I hope these don't spoil the intent of my message for you.

While this project is directed specifically toward parents, it is my hope that many pediatric SLPs and other early intervention professionals will benefit from my explicit "How To's" listed here. How I wish this manual had been available when I started to practice!

The gender pronouns he/she and him/her are alternated throughout the book to represent all of the little people we work with and love.

A Word to Therapists....

When you were growing up, if someone had told you that you'd get paid to sit on the floor and play with babies all day, would you have believed them? I still have to pinch myself some days to believe it's true. Don't we have a great job?

With this great job comes enormous responsibility, and I believe that's the hard part of what we do. It's not easy to help parents understand the scope of a child's developmental delay. It's not easy to teach parents how to help a toddler who is struggling to learn to interact and communicate. It's certainly not easy to first establish that emotional connection with those difficult-to-reach children ourselves. As early interventionists in this day and age, those things have become a large part of what we do. I don't know about you, but they didn't teach me how to do all of those things in grad school!

Like you, the bulk of my training has come on the job during what sometimes feels more like "trial by fire" in homes with real toddlers and real families. Just like our little friends, we seem to learn best by "doing." I hope this therapy manual gives you new things to "do" in sessions with your youngest clients. More importantly, I hope it becomes a way to help you teach parents what to "do" at home between those weekly appointments.

For some of you, who are just beginning your career, the activities and games included here may be new ideas. For some of you, it may mean tweaking the strategies you've used for years or putting a fresh, new spin on what's become routine for you. For some of you, reading these pages may be confirmation that you're doing things right. For all of you, my wish is that this manual will become a useful resource as you continue to work with young children and their families.

A Word to Parents...

When I first began my practice as a pediatric speech-language pathologist, I wished for a crystal ball so that I could tell parents the exact moment their child would begin to talk. I wanted to be able to look them in the eye and say with certainty that after x amount of time, their son or daughter would for sure, without a doubt, learn how to communicate.

Years later, I still don't have that crystal ball, and I can't always make predictions about when a child will say his or her first words, but I do know and tell parents this: until a child learns to interact with others, there's very little chance he'll begin to talk.

I'm always startled by what a revelation this is for some parents, and even worse, some professionals. When I meet a child and it's obvious to me within the first few minutes that he is very difficult to engage and doesn't understand very much of what's said to him, I'm still surprised when his mom, full of anticipation and hope leans forward with wide-eyes and shares that her pediatrician says that her little boy is not talking because he's stubborn, or because he's not around other kids, or that any day now, he'll wake up one morning speaking in full sentences. I wonder to myself, "*Is that doctor not seeing what I'm seeing? Did he notice this child has no sustained interest in other people?*"

After spending more time with that mom and trying my best to administer a standardized test to a toddler who couldn't care less that I'm in the room, I swallow the lump in my throat, grip my well-worn test manual with white knuckles, and try my best not to tear up, as I deliver the words that will confirm her worst fears. Her little boy isn't likely to talk anytime soon.

Neither will any other child who's like him. A child who isn't interested in being with or communicating with other people for most of any given day isn't developmentally ready to understand and use words.

Social interaction is the foundation for meaningful language. Without it, no matter how many words a child can say, there's no real communication. Until a young child gains the desire and ability to connect with his parents in hundreds of shared and mutually enjoyable experiences, his chances of learning to consistently communicate with you are slim to none.

Many times parents don't want to believe this. They think their child is purposefully choosing not to talk, is bored with the world around him, is preoccupied thinking about other things, or is too busy to pay attention to what they're trying to teach him. Or they're convinced that because he looks at and seeks out at least one of his parents during a time of distress that he's "social." They have decided that it really doesn't matter that he only responds to his parents or his siblings, but not his grandparents or the neighbor across the street. The one fleeting moment of catching a stranger's eye in the grocery store and managing a brief hint of a smile does count as "establishing and maintaining eye contact" and "responding to others," doesn't it? Isn't that enough? Won't he just some how, in some way, begin to speak any day now?

My answer is still, *nope*. Even if he does manage to pop out a word, he may not be able to repeat that same word tomorrow, use that word to ask for something he needs, or respond with that word to answer to a question.

Some parents believe that their child is holding out on them and could talk if he wanted to talk. They describe this child as "stubborn" and think if they can somehow wear him down enough, he'll begin to use words. When I meet parents who feel this way, I try to redirect the focus and tell them what I've come to believe. It's not that your child *won't* talk, it's that he *can't* talk.

Making a distinction between *can't* and *won't* is very important, and I beg moms and dads of the children that I work with on my caseload to see the difference and change the way they think about their child's delay. Without even meaning to, we treat a child differently when we view developmental issues from a *behavioral* perspective. In our minds when we're thinking, "He could say this word if he wanted to talk," or "She won't listen to me no matter what I try," we throw up our hands and walk away.

If you happen to be an aggressive person yourself, you might push and push and push your child so that teaching him to talk has turned into a power struggle, an all out show-down and battle of wills. Instead of enjoying each other during your time together, you've both ended up frustrated.

When we change our thinking and view a child's missed milestones as something he *can't* do vs. something he *won't* do, we begin to try to help him, and look for a solution to the problem.

When a kid *can* talk, he will talk. It makes life so much easier, for him and for you! Once a child begins to come together socially (he wants to interact with you), cognitively (he understands and attaches meaning to your words and can follow your directions), neurologically (he can plan and send the message he wants to convey), and physiologically (he can physically produce speech sounds), he will learn how to talk.

This book is about the earliest piece and foundation of that process. All communication begins with being social. Once a child learns to love being with you, he forms the foundation necessary to help him understand and use language.

Many professionals have written extensively about using relationships and emotional connections as the underlying theory in the treatment of children with social communication delays. For more specific information, the authors I suggest are listed in Chapter 6, References and Recommended Reading.

Helping your child learn to play WITH you is a huge first step in helping him learn how to communicate. It's not always easy, but it can be very, very rewarding. When you begin to see your child smile and light up when he recognizes one of the new games you'll teach him, when his eyes twinkle as he anticipates playing that game with you, and when you both begin to truly have FUN sharing a song or toy together, you'll know you're well on your way.

The simple routines and games that are included in this book are designed to inspire you to play with your child and to motivate your child to play with you. It's a book of ideas to get you started so that you'll know what to do when you play. You'll learn ways to interact with your child with step-by-step instructions for each play routine. You'll also learn how to gauge your child's responses, what "goals" to set for your child, and how to expand each game so that your child keeps moving forward. Finally, in chapter 5, Solutions for Problems during Play, you'll find suggestions for new things to try when what you're doing isn't working.

I don't want you to read this book; I want you to USE this book. Here's how I recommend you begin. Flip through the initial pages of the first chapter, Easiest Beginner Routines. Pick one or two new routines you'll introduce *today* as you play. In a couple of days when your child begins to respond to these, add two new routines so that you have a repertoire of four social games she can play. After that, add a couple of more so that you now share six games. Keep building over the next few weeks until your child can play many of these games, and preferably during one long episode of play with you.

Your initial goal is for your child to work up to playing these kinds of games with you for at least 10 minutes at a time, <u>many </u>times a day. You can play one single game during this time if your child likes it. Even though 10 minutes doesn't seem like that long, most of us (including me!), want to play a few different social games or sing several songs during this time period.

 This <u>10 minute period</u> is sometimes easier to achieve when playing with toys. With toys, your goal is to work up to at least <u>10 minutes per toy</u> before moving on to something new.

For some children, your change in approach will be enough to accomplish this goal in the first few days or weeks. For other children, it may be several weeks or even a couple of months before he's happily playing with you for this length of time.

Once she is consistently playing with you for 10 minutes, expand that playtime to 15 minutes at a time, several times a day. When she can do that, bump it up to 20 minutes at a time, in several 1:1 play sessions, over the course of your day together.

I don't want to freak you out or anything when you read this next statement, so get ready for what could be a bombshell. Experts advise that a child with social and language delays should spend most of his or her day "engaged" in meaningful activity with an adult. The formal recommendation based on research is that in order for a parent to expect that a child could make such significant progress that he's caught up to what's "normal" for his age, the young child should spend 20 to 25 hours a week engaged in 1:1 playtime with an adult. That's about 3 hours a day in direct interaction with an adult.

Wow! No matter how you divide it up over the week, that's a big time commitment, for him and for you. Watching TV with you (which is <u>not</u> <u>recommended</u> <u>at</u> <u>all</u> for children with social communication delays), playing with his toys on the floor with an occasional comment from a parent sitting on the couch, or just hangin' around while mom is busy going about her day doesn't count toward that 20-25 hours per week of interaction.

Interestingly, activities such as playing alone in a room or watching movie after movie are the kinds of things that most very young children with typically developing communication skills *don't* like to do for very long. Toddlers with typically developing social and language skills *demand* attention. They often put up such a fuss that their moms can't stay on the phone too long, visit the restroom alone, or wash the dishes without the child being included. A child with typically developing language often won't tolerate being gated away in a separate play room while his mom is in the kitchen making dinner. This child insists that he or she go too! Their persistence isn't always with words. Children with typically developing language skills frequently initiate contact with their moms and dads, even if they're not saying much of anything yet. Using their gestures, facial expressions, and early vocalizations, they demand constant interaction. This is one of the main qualitative differences between a child who develops language as expected and one who doesn't and falls behind.

Parents with a child with social and language difficulties must go out of their way to engage that child in play and during every day routines. I've used the word "engaged" several times without explaining it, so let me do that in case this is a new term for you. *Engagement* means that your child is totally involved with what you're *both* doing and saying. He exhibits *joint attention*, meaning that he is focused on the object you're talking about *and* you. He looks back and forth between the toy and your face. He hangs on your every word. He takes a turn, even without words, in your "conversation" since he smiles in shared joy and shakes his head in response to what you say. He's not distracted by a commercial on TV, the ceiling fan, or the shadow from the sun shining in the window. He doesn't roam away uninterested. There's no doubt that he's heard you or understood you. He's 100% there, fully participating in what you're teaching him. If you wanted to stop the conversation and walk away to do something else, you couldn't, because you feel so intimately connected to him, and that feeling is obviously and eagerly returned from him to you.

When I describe that kind of interaction to many parents, they wonder aloud, "How do I accomplish this with my child?" Whether you are close to that experience now, very far away, or somewhere in the middle, you can get there. First you have to find a way to teach your child that it's more fun to be with mommy or daddy than anything else he could possibly do.

For a young child, this means meeting him wherever he is and then helping him develop the next highest level of interaction. For a child with severe social deficits, his first goal might be just stopping his own activity and looking your way. For a child who is already responding with attention, the goal would be participating in what you're doing, first with a smile, and then with some kind of gesture or action to "join" in your game. For a child who can stay with you for a few minutes during a song, the goal might be for her to begin the same song next time in whatever way she can.

I believe that most children, even those with significant social and language delays, can and do get better, no matter where they are developmentally, when a parent makes a determined and focused effort to help. Taking a child to a professional for therapy, participating in an early intervention program, or enrolling him in a special school is essential for a child with developmental delays, but in my experience, the children who make the most progress are the ones with committed parents who take on the responsibility of being their child's first and best teacher.

To accomplish this with a toddler or preschooler, the most important requirement is not that you have an advanced degree, but that you become the most reliable, most consistently present, most FUN person your child has ever seen.

This doesn't necessarily mean that you are loud, out of control, or so far from your normal personality that your child won't recognize you, but it does mean that you are the most playful, the most entertaining, and I'll say it again, the most FUN mom or dad you can possibly be.

For some parents, play doesn't come naturally, and this kind of interaction is a real stretch. In therapy sessions when I demonstrate for them how I want them to play with their child with delays, they say things like, "I don't have that much energy," "That's just not me," or "I'd be embarrassed if I acted that way."

My response is sometimes hard for them to hear. *How's what you're already doing working out for you?*

You're going to have to do things differently if you want your child to improve. If he were going to talk on his own doing the things you already do, he wouldn't have a social or communication delay, and it's highly unlikely you'd be reading this book.

Don't get me wrong. I am absolutely **not** blaming parents for a child's developmental issues. Most of the time delays are <u>not</u> due to something a mom did while she was pregnant (unless there was drug or alcohol abuse) or even something parents have or haven't done since the child was born. Some children are born with differences diagnosed before or at birth such as Down Syndrome or in the first few months of life such as cerebral palsy. Problems might be present at birth, but they're not detected until the child begins to fall behind. Many times delays are due to the way a child is "wired." Neurologically he was "predisposed" to have some difficulties. Developmental delays can also be inherited. If mom or dad were late talkers or had learning difficulties, chances are, one of their children will too. Sometimes no matter how many different specialists you see, you never find *the* reason your child is not developing normally. You obviously can't control any of those things, and even if you were given the chance, you wouldn't change your sweet, sweet baby you've so come to love as your very own.

The advice I give parents is to move on to what you can do now and change the circumstances you can control. The best way a parent can help a child learn to interact is to help him *want* to interact. The child needs the initial desire to communicate with you. How do you create that desire? I've already told you. You have to become the most playful, most consistently present, most FUN person your child has ever seen.

Since you've bought this book, you've probably visited my website at teachmetotalk.com. While there I hope you've purchased or at least watched the clips from my DVDs. Sometimes it's easier to SEE someone else be playful and then know how to implement this approach with your child, rather than reading about it. The intention of this manual is to expand the basic strategies you've learned from the DVDs and give you many, many more ideas to use as you carry out those basic techniques with your own child.

Even though you're reading this instead of meeting with me in your home, I'll go ahead and give you the same advice I give almost every parent I work with when we begin speech therapy with a young child. During play with you is when your child is going to make the most initial progress improving his social and language skills. Since I'll never get to see you in action with your child, go ahead and assume that you too are like most parents in the beginning phase of therapy. You're probably not playing as much as you should or being as animated as you need to be during playtime with your child. As I frequently say to parents and other therapists, **RATCHET IT UP A NOTCH!**

Start with what you think is your most exciting, most energetic, most playful, most loving, warmest, friendliest voice and demeanor, and then move up a level from there to begin. Your goal is to woo your child, to pull him in, to make him want to connect with you more than anything else he could do at the moment. It may seem over the top, it may seem like way too much, but most of the time for children with social delays, it's what it takes to make a real breakthrough. You have to get her attention. You have to be more interesting for him to watch than Sponge Bob, the garbage truck outside, Thomas' wheels, or the fuzz blowing across the floor. It has to be worth it for him to give up the other "thing" that's captured and held his attention.

You have a huge advantage over any other person that would try to entice your child in this way. You are your baby's mommy or daddy. You are your kid's #1 fan. You are THE person your child can count on, no matter what, day in and day out. Nobody understands your child and knows your child like you do. No doctor, no therapist, not even a trusted and beloved nanny or teacher.

I'll even go one further. Although I'm very good with children, I'm no match for you with your own child. You already have that connection to your child. Now it's up to you to teach your child how to make that connection *with* you. No one else can do that quite like you. Are you ready to get started? Then keep reading!

Easiest Beginner Social Routines

Young children with social and language delays best learn how to interact with others during the structure of a "game." A child who is running around the room or sitting alone looking at a toy may not respond to his mother when she calls his name, but watch what happens if she changes her approach. When she begins to sing a song or say a little rhyme, her child stops what he's doing and hints that he's starting to listen to her. The next time his mom starts to sing that same song, he looks to find her. After 2 or 3 more repetitions, he might actually give his mother a smile. As his mom continues their new game over the next several days, he slowly begins to try to play too, in his own way. A social routine is born.

Start with the routines here if your child has no or few "games" he can play. Each of the following 23 activities initially requires little participation on your child's part, other than a pause to look at you and that he let you help him perform the game. Hopefully, as you "play" the game over and over, you'll see his attention to you expand and then blossom into a true social response. Once he's reacting to you, he'll then begin to happily participate, and then finally, you'll help teach him ways to initiate the game he now knows and loves!

On each page you'll find:

- The name of the game
- Materials required (if any)
- Description of a child's preferences to help you decide if this game is a good place to begin with your child
- Detailed instructions in "How to Play"
- Key words YOU should say to elicit your child's sounds and words
- List of child's goals so that you'll know what responses to shoot for, how to help your child move to a more advanced response, and how to measure progress
- Problem solving tips specific to each game
- Ideas for expanding the game and new games to try when your child has mastered the first one

If your child doesn't seem to enjoy a particular game in your first few attempts, don't give up! I sometimes play a game 5 or 6 times each session for several weeks in therapy before a child gives me any indication he likes the game. Keep at it. Repetition builds familiarity, and once a child recognizes the game, he's more likely to want to play.

Teach Me To Play WITH You

Let me also interject that what YOU say during these games is important. I've included the same key words and play sounds I use when I play these games during speech therapy. Play sounds, or exclamatory words, like whee, wow, whoa, uh-oh, boom, oops, and yay, and other sounds we use in play, such as animal sounds or vehicle noises, are often easier for a child who tunes out speech to attend to and then try to imitate. Most of these words are easy to pronounce too, so they give a child a better shot at success when you're working to get those first word attempts. Even though these may not seem like "words" at all, they are! As I tell parents I work with, if you can spell it, it's a word! Those play sounds are made up of the same consonant and vowel sequences needed to pronounce other "real" words, so by introducing these kinds of words, you are helping your child acquire new sounds and lay the foundation for speech and language to develop.

Occasionally parents get so caught up in being more playful that they overwhelm a child with too many different words or long sentences. When this happens, the child retreats or shuts down. To avoid this problem, think about what you're saying during play. Make your own words count. Use simple words and short phrases. Use a sing-song or melodic voice to capture your child's attention. Repeat your key words and short phrases over and over. Don't be so afraid of saying the wrong thing that you're too quiet, but make sure what you do say are words that your child can understand and hopefully be able to repeat.

Remember that your overall mission is to first teach your child to love playing *with* you. Even though I've listed specific instructions here, the most significant goal is for your child to connect with you and enjoy playtime with his favorite person. If you mess up the words, or forget a step, or even if your child comes up with his or her own unique response, who cares? Keep going! The important thing is to have FUN! Make these games your own!

One last word of advice, get ready to play! Turn off your phone and the TV. Ignore any other distractions. Plaster a big, warm smile on your face and get ready to woo your baby into interacting with you. He's waiting...

GIVE ME 5

Materials: None

Great for a Child Who:
Has no or few other "games" he can play

How to Play:
Hold your hand up in front of your child and happily say, **"Give me 5!"** If he doesn't reach out to slap your hand after a few tries, ask another adult or older child to demonstrate. Say to the other person, "Give me 5!" and then say, "Yay" or "Alright" after the person slaps your palm.

If your toddler still doesn't respond by slapping your palm, use your other hand to grab his hand and make him slap your palm. You may have another person stand behind him to take his hand and make him slap your open palm.

Smile and say, "Yay!" or "Alright!" after he "gives you 5" each time. Gradually provide less assistance until he can do this trick each time you ask.

Child's Goals:
Of course the #1 goal is for your child to have fun and to complete the game by hitting your hand. You're also looking for consistent, sustained eye contact and smiles while you're playing this game.

To help him initiate this game, begin this game whenever you see him with an open palm. Slap his open hand saying, "Give me 5!" and "Yay," or "Alright!"

Don't forget to play this over and over with lots of repetitions so he "learns" the game. As with all of our play routines, eventually your child should play this game several times in a row before moving on to another game or toy with you during your 1:1 play time.

Expand the Game:
1. Play with a new person. Have dad, a grandparent, or the older kid next door initiate and play the "Give Me 5" game with your child.

2. This is a great game you can play while waiting in line at the grocery store, sitting at a stop light, or anywhere else when you need a distraction for your child.

BLOWING BELLIES

<u>Materials</u>: None

<u>Great for a Child Who</u>:
Has no or few other "games" he can play
Frequently lies on his back
Likes tickling on her tummy
Likes roughhousing
Frequently ignores or avoids you

<u>How to Play</u>:
Lay your child down on his back, or when he's already in that position, creep toward him and say,

Get......
Your......
Belly!!! (Or "tummy" if this is what you already say.)

Then lift up his shirt and blow on his stomach.

Most babies, toddlers, and even older children love this game with their parents.

<u>Child's Goals</u>:
Your first goal is for your child to have fun and want to play this game over and over. You're looking for consistent, sustained eye contact and "belly" laughs of sheer delight while you're playing.

The next goal is for your child to anticipate that you're going to blow on her stomach. You can see this when she begins to smile and grab her belly or shirt.

Eventually we want your child to "ask" for this game before you start another turn by grabbing his belly or holding up his shirt while looking at you. Eye contact is a form of initiation!

Toddlers learn through repetition. Young children with difficulty paying attention need even more repetition. Play this game over and over throughout the day so that he "learns" the game.

As with all of our play routines, eventually your child should play this game several times in a row before moving on to another game or toy with you during your 1:1 play time.

Expand the Game:

1. Play with a new person. Have dad or a grandparent initiate and play the game in the same way you do. To initiate the game you say, "Grandma's gonna get your belly!"

2. Begin play from a greater distance away from your child. Start the play routine from across the room. When she happens to glance at you, say, "Belly?" and make a blowing sound as you move across the room to get her. Then launch into your routine with, "Get….. Your……" This trains her to look at you and for you, even from across the room. Many children with social delays need help and motivation to establish and maintain eye contact with people when they're up close and with people from a distance. Build both kinds of opportunities for practice into your play routines.

3. When you see her rubbing her belly or touching her shirt at other times, initiate the game by saying, "Belly? Want me to get your belly?" This will help her learn to initiate the game on her own. Then drop everything else you're doing and begin the routine.

4. Sometimes this game can be a great distraction if you're about to "lose" your child or you sense a meltdown might be coming. Be sure to stop the game if it seems to make the tantrum worse.

5. As with tickling, some children won't enjoy this kind of play or touch. Find just the right balance to make it fun for your child. You might try giving kisses instead of blowing on her belly. Or pretend to eat your child's tummy saying, "Yum, yum, yum!" Your goal is to get a positive reaction, so try different things until you do get a full-blown, joyful response.

6. If your child is talking or beginning to try to imitate words, wait for her to say "belly" or even "be" for belly or "tu" for tummy before you blow on her stomach. This may be something you won't hear for a few months, but keep trying by modeling a word she could say.

PEEK - A - BOO

<u>Materials</u>: Blanket

<u>Great for a Child Who:</u>
Has no or few other "games" he can play
Uses a blanket as her comfort object

<u>How to Play</u>:
Cover your child's head with the blanket and then ask, **"Where's _____?"** Ask several times and build anticipation with your voice.

Jerk the blanket off with a big gesture and say, "Boo!" Specifically say, "Boo," rather than "Peek-a-boo," "Pee-pie," or even, "There she is," because "Boo" is a word your toddler is more likely to be able to say.

<u>Child's Goals:</u>
Watch his responses. We want him to connect with you by looking at you, smiling, and laughing when you remove the blanket. If he doesn't laugh, be more fun! Smile bigger! Squeal! Increase your own level of energy, animation, and excitement. Try a tickle or jiggle to get him going.

After a while, we want her to move or giggle in anticipation that you are going to take the blanket off her head.

Next we want him to try to remove the blanket by himself. Help him if he gets stuck.

After a few days playing this game, we want her to try to cover her own head when you give her the blanket to begin the game.

You can help him learn to initiate the game by saying, "Where's _____" when his head is even partially covered with a blanket at other times during the day.

An indication that he's really "learned" the game comes when he initiates the game with you by reaching out on his own to get a blanket and then covering and uncovering himself. Place a blanket in front of him and ask, "Play boo?" If he doesn't pick it up, point to the blanket so that he learns to get the blanket by himself to begin the game.

Toddlers learn through repetition. Young children with difficulty paying attention need even more repetition. Play this game over and over throughout the day with several repetitions each time so that he "learns" the game.

Saying "Boo" might not come right away, but if she's doing all of the other parts, we know she's understanding the routine, with or without the word. Keep trying to elicit this word by saying, "Boo" many times during play to help her learn to imitate you. Once you've played this game many times for several days, pause just before you say, "Boo!" Smile and look expectantly at your child as if to indicate that it's her turn to say "Boo!" Since you've played this game many, many times now and she knows what comes next, your child may surprise you and say it on her own!

As with all of our play routines, eventually your child should play this game several times in a row before moving on to another game or toy with you during your 1:1 play time.

Expand the Game:

1. Hide under the blanket, and let your child take the blanket off your head. Say, "Where's Mommy?" If your child doesn't try to uncover you, uncover yourself. Better yet, have someone else help your child take the blanket off your head to teach him that he can do this part of the game.

2. Get a new person to play either role by being the person who hides or calls the child as he hides.

3. Play with another obstacle. Hide behind a pillow, a door, behind the shower curtain during bath, or behind the couch when your child is playing nearby. Call your child as you did before saying, "Where's _____?" Or ask your child, "Where's Mommy?" Then pop out and say, "Boo!"

4. When your child masters this game and can cover and uncover her own head easily, introduce the next activity, "Where Oh Where."

WHERE OH WHERE?

Materials: Blanket

Great for a Child Who:
Uses a blanket as her comfort object
Plays Peek-A-Boo well

How to Play:
This is a more advanced version of Peek-A-Boo, but one that older toddlers and young preschoolers love.

Place the blanket over your child's head and sing to the tune of "Ten Little Indians,"

Where, oh where, oh where is (child's name)?
>   (Hold both hands out palms facing up and move them up and down as if asking, "Where is it?")

Where, oh where, oh where is (child's name)?
>   (Continue same hand motions.)

Where, oh where, oh where is (child's name)?
>   (Same)

Where can (child's name) be?

After a pause, call your child's name and wait for her to come out. Say, "Boo!" when she uncovers her head. Help her with the blanket if she doesn't come out on her own.

Repeat giving your child as many turns as she will take.

Child's Goals:
As with Peek-A-Boo, we initially want to watch for his responses. We want him to connect with you by looking at you, smiling, and laughing when you remove the blanket. If he doesn't laugh, be more fun! Smile bigger! Squeal! Increase your own level of animation and excitement. Use your voice to indicate you're having FUN!

If she tries to take the blanket off too early, help her stay under a little longer until you finish the song, but don't ruin the mood by scolding her.

Next we want to see her try to cover her own head when you give her the blanket to begin the game, sit covered for the whole song, and then uncover herself for the ending.

An indication that he's really "learned" the game comes when he initiates the game with you by reaching out on his own to get a blanket to begin the game.

Saying "Boo" might not come right away, but if she's doing all of the other parts, we know she's understanding the routine, with or without the word.

After several days of playing, many children begin to try to sing, "Where oh where," so listen carefully for an attempt.

Toddlers learn through repetition. Young children with difficulty paying attention need even more repetition. Play this game over and over throughout the day with several repetitions each time so that he "learns" the game.

As with all of our play routines, eventually your child should play this game several times in a row before moving on to another game or toy with you during your 1:1 play time.

Expand the Game:

1. Add another new person to your game so your child can see you sing and do these hand motions. This is a great game for adding Dad, grandparents, siblings, and same-age friends.

2. You hide and sing, "Where, oh where, oh where is Mommy?" You may need someone else to help him stay for the entire song.

3. You can begin to use this song as way to call your child, especially if he doesn't normally respond to his name. Once he's learned the song and played it with you for several days, use it to get his attention when he's farther away from you, but in the same room. It will teach him to listen for his name and come to you when you call him in this fun way. Once he's responding to this, try it from another room to see if he's listening and will come to find you when you call him. Be sure to scoop him up with a huge smile, a big hug, and a kiss so that he knows you're ecstatic that he responded.

4. This is a great circle time activity for a small playgroup. It's an entertaining way to teach turn-taking and helps young children learn their little friends' names.

AH...BOOM!

<u>Materials</u>: Flat surface to pat such as a chair, the couch, a low table, or your bed

<u>Great for a Child Who:</u>
Has no or few other "games" he can play
Is just beginning to try to clap when he sees someone else clap

<u>How to Play</u>:
When your child is looking in your direction, begin with your arms outstretched toward the ground, and then raise your arms slowly over your head as you build anticipation with your voice saying,

"Aaaaaaaaaah....

BOOM!"
     (Quickly lower your arms and hit the surface in front of you with both hands.)

Say, "Boom, boom, boom, boom!" several times as you continue to hit the surface with both of your hands.

After a few seconds, clap and say, "Yay!"

Begin the routine again.

I often play this game when I'm seated on the floor and a child is across a table or twin bed from me. There's something very alluring about being eye level with a child and both using the same simple actions during play. Having an adult "hit" a table and use a word like "boom" is also very inviting for some children who may not have seen a grown-up play like this before.

<u>Child's Goals:</u>
Your first goal is for your child to watch you as you play this game several times. Many children don't smile or laugh until you've done this routine several times, so be sure you're smiling and look like you're having the time of your life while you're playing this very simple, but enticing game.

The next goal is for your child to begin to participate by copying your actions. Children usually begin to pat (or hit) the floor or the same surface you're using with both hands as you continue to say, "Boom, boom, boom!" If he doesn't, gently take his hands and help him pat the surface as you say, "Boom, boom, boom!" Provide as little assistance as necessary so that he will begin to do this action on his own.

Next we'd like for your child to raise his arms in the beginning and then clap at the end of the game too.

Many children will begin to try to imitate the word, "Boom" during this game, or even the beginning sound, "Aaaah." If I can't get a child to imitate, "Aaaah," I try what SLPs call "audible inhalation." In plain English, use your voice as you inhale.

Imitating gestures, sounds, and play words like these during a game is a HUGE step in learning to imitate real words. This routine is often the very first time I see and hear a child directly try to imitate a gesture, sound, or word during therapy. It's simple enough for even the most elusive child to want to play. If you've had very little luck with previous games, give this one a try.

Toddlers learn through repetition. Young children with difficulty paying attention need even more repetition. Play this game over and over throughout the day with several repetitions each time so that he "learns" the game.

As with all of our play routines, eventually your child should play this game several times in a row before moving on to another game or toy with you during your 1:1 play time.

Expand the Game:
1. Add another new person to your game so that your child can see someone else playing with you and imitating these motions and words. This is a great game for adding Dad, grandparents, siblings, and same-age friends.

2. This is another fun, easy game you can play virtually anywhere. Try it when your child is seated in his high chair at home or in a restaurant. Or try it in the bathtub when you don't mind getting splashed.

3. Begin the game from a greater distance away so that you're teaching your child to seek you out to play. After he likes and has learned the game over several days, begin the game when he's well across the room. When he's mastered the game, try beginning when he's in another room to see if he's listening and will come find you to play.

TICKLE FINGERS

<u>Materials</u>: None

<u>Great for a Child Who:</u>
Has no or few other "games" he can play
Likes tickling on her tummy or other body parts
Frequently ignores or avoids you
Runs away from you

<u>How to Play</u>:
Begin this game when you are a few feet away from your child. If you're up close, lean back to begin so that it looks like you're getting closer with every word. Wiggle your fingers like you're tickling and pause between every word to build anticipation as you walk or lean closer and closer to your child and say,

Here....
Come.....
Tickle Fingers!
Tickle, tickle, tickle!!!
> (Laugh and tickle your child's tummy.)

<u>Child's Goals</u>:
Of course the #1 goal is for your child to have fun and want to continue this game over and over. You're looking for sustained eye contact and sheer joy while you're playing.

The next goal is for your child to anticipate that you're going to tickle her. You can see this when she begins to grab her belly or shirt and giggle. Watch for eye contact since this is a way for her to continue or initiate the game. A smile, even as she slightly turns away, may be a tease and "request" for you to play again.

Eventually we want a child to initiate and "ask" for this game before you start another turn by grabbing her belly or lifting her shirt while looking at you. Pause before beginning another turn to see if she will use a gesture like this to "request" that you continue.

Another goal might be for a child to wiggle his fingers, lean, or reach toward you to continue or initiate the game.

If a child is talking or imitating words, wait for her to say, "Tickle" or even "Ti" before tickling her.

Don't forget to play this game over and over throughout the day with several repetitions each time so he "learns" the game. As with all of our play routines, eventually your child should play this game several times in a row before moving on to another game or toy with you during your 1:1 play time.

Expand the Game:

1. Play with a new person. Have dad or grandma initiate and play the game in the same way you do. You might even ask your child, "Daddy? Want tickles from Daddy?" as a way to begin the game.

2. Begin the game from a greater distance away from your child. Start the play routine from across the room. When she happens to glance at you, say, "Tickles? Want tickles?" and wiggle your fingers like you're going to tickle her. Then launch into your routine with, "Here….. Come……" This trains her to look at you and for you, even from across the room. Many children with social delays need help and motivation to establish and maintain eye contact with people when they're up close and with people from a distance. Build both kinds of opportunities for practice into your routines.

3. When you see her rubbing her tummy or touching her shirt at other times, initiate the game by saying, "Tickles? Want tickles?" This will help her learn to initiate the game on her own with a gesture like this. Drop everything else you're doing and begin the routine.

4. Sometimes this game can be a great distraction if you're about to "lose" your child or you sense a meltdown might be coming. Be sure to stop if it seems to make it worse.

5. Some children don't enjoy tickling. Find just the right balance to make it fun for your child. Light touch is often far more aversive to sensory defensive children than deep pressure, so a flat palm and a firm "jiggle" to your child's belly may be more fun. Some toddlers may prefer tickles under their arms or on their legs. Your goal is to get a positive reaction, so try different ways and places of tickling until you get a full-blown, joyful response.

6. Expand your child's imagination by using this same tickle motion and pretending to be a "spider," "bug," or "monster." Pick anything you think your child will find amusing. You can say, "Here….. Comes…..a……MONSTER!" Then tickle your child with a big "monster" laugh.

THIS LITTLE PIGGY

<u>Materials</u>: Bare feet!

<u>Great for a Child Who:</u>
Has no or few other "games" he can play
Likes tickles to her tummy or other body parts
Frequently lies on his back
Grabs her toes often
May ignore or avoid you

<u>How to Play</u>:
Begin by holding your child's foot in one hand and using your other hand to do the following actions while you say,

This little piggy went to market.
> (Wiggle big toe.)

This little piggy stayed home.
> (Wiggle second toe.)

This little piggy had roast beef.
> (Wiggle third toe.)

This little piggy had none.
> (Wiggle fourth toe.)

And this little piggy cried, "Wee, wee, wee,"
> (Wiggle little toe.)

All the way home.
> (Tickle up child's leg to his belly.)

Child's Goals:

As with the other games, we initially want to watch for her responses. We want her to connect with you by looking at you, smiling, and laughing, especially by the time you get to her little toe!

An early goal is for him to stay with you the entire game.

Another goal would be for her to move her foot toward you when you ask, "Piggies?" or or even teasingly hide her foot when you say, "I'm gonna get your piggies!"

An indication that he's *really* learned the game would be for him to remove his socks and/or shoes when you ask him if he wants to play "Piggies?"

Toddlers learn through repetition. Children with difficulty paying attention need even more repetition. Play this game over and over throughout the day with several repetitions each time so that he "learns" the game.

As with all of our play routines, eventually your child should play this game several times in a row before moving on to another game or toy with you during your 1:1 play time.

Expand the Game:

1. Play the game with a new person. This game is a classic, so chances are your child's grandparents and even older children will know how to play. Help a new person initiate this game with your child and play the same way you do.

2. This is a fun game to play when you're snuggling and want to keep your child close to you, but don't tickle so hard that it makes him want to get away!

3. Expand the game by changing the ending and saying, "I'm gonna EAT your piggies!" Then make lots of eating noises by saying, "Chomp! Chomp! Chomp!" or "Yum! Yum! Yum!" as you pretend to eat his toes!

4. Alternate this game with the previous activity, "Here Come Tickle Fingers" if your child likes both games.

CHOO-CHOO SONG

(Adapted from Kate Hensler, DI)

<u>Materials</u>: None

<u>Great for a Child Who</u>:

Has no or few other "games" he can play

Frequently lies down on his back

Loves trains

Ignores or avoids you – *especially* when he's playing with his trains

<u>How to Play</u>:

When your child is on his back, hold his feet or his ankles and push his legs toward his tummy, and then pull them back out straight. Push and pull his legs rhythmically like a train's wheels rolling as you chant,

Here comes the choo-choo train chuggin' down the track,

Chugga-chugga- chugga- chugga,

Chugga-chugga- chugga- chugga,

Chugga-chugga- chugga- chugga,

Choo-choo!

> (Let go of your child's legs and reach up with one arm as if you're pulling a train's whistle to sign "choo-choo." After I've played this game a couple of times, I grab the child's arm to help him sign as I say, "Choo-choo!" Then follow up with a big tickle or hug.)

You could change the motions by pulling your child around on the floor by his legs (Some kids LOVE this!) during the Chugga-chugga part, then stop suddenly and grab or tickle him for "Choo-choo!"

Child's Goals:

As with the other games, we initially want to watch for his responses. We want him to connect with you by looking at you, smiling, and laughing.

An early goal is for him to stay with you through the entire game.

Another goal would be for him to hold up his legs to you when he's lying down when you ask, "Choo-choo?"

You know he's *really* learned the game when he lies down when you ask him if he wants to play choo-choos, or if you see him holding up his legs when you're approaching him as if to invite you to play.

Eventually your child may say or sign, "Choo-choo" when you say this at the end of the game, or as a request to ask you to play this very fun game!

Toddlers learn through repetition. Young children with difficulty paying attention need even more repetition. Play this game over and over throughout the day with several repetitions each time so that he "learns" the game.

As with all of our play routines, eventually your child should play this game several times in a row before moving on to another game or toy with you during your 1:1 play time.

Expand the Game:

1. Play the game with a new person. This is a new game, so you'll want to have the other person watch you a few times so that they can play the game exactly like you do.

2. This is a good way to make playing with trains much more social for a child who's obsessed with his trains and finds it hard to share or attend to someone else. It's also another way to get him off his tummy if he spends lots of time there watching the wheels spin. Flip him over to his back and begin the game.

UP DOWN!

<u>Materials</u>: None

<u>Great for a Child Who:</u>
Has no or few other "games" she can play
Will sit on your lap and hold your hands for at least a short time
Likes to be held, but really doesn't "connect" with you when you hold him
Likes movement/bouncing games
Likes to crash into objects or fall down

<u>How to Play</u>:
Sit down on the floor with your legs outstretched in front of you, and seat your child on your knees facing you. Hold your child's hands. Lift your child up on your knees saying,

Up..... Up.... Up.....
        (Slowly lift up your knees on each word and build anticipation with your voice.)
Down!
        (Quickly lower your legs flat touching the floor.)

Experiment to see how fast or slow your child likes for you to raise and lower your legs. Most children like the slower pace going up and prefer a fast-paced, crash-landing on the floor as a big surprise for "down."

<u>Child's Goals:</u>
Watch for her response to this game. We want her to connect with you and enjoy your time playing. You can see this by a smile, increased eye contact, and hopefully, even a "twinkle" in her eyes.

If he doesn't respond positively, be more fun! Increase your own level of animation. Try a big hug after "down" to get him laughing and smiling.

Vary your speed or the number of times you say, "Up – up" to find what your child likes best. For a child who won't stay in one place for very long, quickly move to "down."

Another goal for this game would be for him to reach for your hands as you hold both palms out and up, as if to invite him to play. Wiggle your fingers toward him as an invitation for him to grab your hands.

After you've played this one for a while, help your child initiate this game with you by putting him on your lap and then asking him if he wants to play by saying, "Up? Up?" but don't hold his hands to begin. Leave your hands in your lap, or even put them behind your back, to see if your child will initiate grabbing your hands to begin.

Toddlers learn through repetition. Children with difficulty paying attention need even more repetition. Play this game over and over throughout the day with several repetitions each time so that he "learns" the game.

As with all of our play routines, eventually your child should play this game several times in a row before moving on to another game or toy with you during your 1:1 play time.

Expand the Game:

1. Play with a new person. Have the person watch you several times to learn how to play the game exactly like you do.

2. After your child likes this game, expand how and where you play. You could play this game by picking your child up from the floor, bed, or chair. Lift him high into the air for "up," and then crash him down on his feet or bottom for "down."

3. If your child seems scared when you lift her up, which is called gravitational insecurity, try the next game, "Humpty Dumpty."

HUMPTY DUMPTY

<u>Materials</u>: None

<u>Great for a Child Who:</u>
Will sit on your lap and hold your hands for at least a short time
Likes to be held, but really doesn't "connect" with you when you hold him
Likes movement/bouncing games
Likes to crash into objects or fall down
Likes the "Up Down" game
Becomes scared when she's lifted up on your knees in the "Up Down" game

<u>How to Play:</u>
Sit on a chair holding your child on your lap. Hold him under his arms and say,

Humpty Dumpty sat on a wall.
> (Bounce him on your lap to the rhythm of your words.)

Humpty Dumpty had a.... great.....big......
> (Bounce more slowly and exaggerate your words.)

FALL!!!
> (Continue to hold under your child under his arms, but open your legs and let him fall through. Some kids like falling all the way to the floor, but most of the time, I just drop a child a few inches below my knees.)

Say, "Yay" as you pull your child back up to your lap and begin again.

<u>Child's Goals:</u>
Your first goal is for your child to stay on your lap for several repetitions of the routine.

Of course you want your child to respond positively to you by maintaining eye contact and smiling while you're playing.

Next you want him to anticipate the "fall" by smiling before you let him drop. This lets you know he remembers what comes next.

After you've played this game for several weeks, your child may begin to say, "Fall," or even "Ah" for fall, if you look at him and pause expectantly just before it's time to say this word.

Toddlers learn through repetition. Young children with difficulty paying attention need even more repetition. Play this game over and over throughout the day with several repetitions each time so that he "learns" the game.

As with all of our play routines, eventually your child should play this game several times in a row before moving on to another game or toy with you during your 1:1 play time.

Expand the Game:

1. Play the game with a new person. Have the person watch you several times to learn how to play the game exactly like you do.

2. Play in a new place. This one is great for the waiting room at the doctor's office or anywhere you're sitting and can bounce and laugh.

3. In her book Giggle Time, Susan Aud Sonders plays a variation of this game where she flips the child over backwards to the floor on "fall." If your child enjoys spinning or somersaults, he'll love this version of the game!

ROCKING, ROCKING

<u>Materials</u>: None

<u>Great for a Child Who</u>:
Has no or few other "games" she can play
Sits on your lap and holds your hands for at least a short time
Likes to be held, but really doesn't "connect" with you when you hold her
Likes movement/bouncing games
Likes to rock
Likes the "Up Down" game
Responds more to music than talking

<u>How to Play</u>:
Sit down on the floor with your legs outstretched in front of you and place your baby on your lap facing you. Hold your baby's hands and rock back and forward as you sing to the tune of "Are You Sleeping" or "Frere Jacques,"

We are rocking,
We are rocking,
Rock, rock, rock,
Rock, rock, rock,
Rocking, rocking, rocking,
Rocking, rocking, rocking,
Now we stop!

<u>Child's Goals</u>:
An initial goal for this game is to get him to stay through the entire song. If he tries to wiggle off your lap, try a more energetic rock. Or change the words to "Bouncing" and sing that version while bouncing him on your legs.

This game is too boring for some toddlers, and if this is the case, move on to a more advanced version of this game with the next routines, "Row Your Boat" and "Ride A Little Horsie."

However, this game is just the right speed for some children, especially ones who can't tolerate lots of language. Sometimes when there are too many different words in a song, children can't process all of that language, and their "Fight or Flight" response kicks in. That's when you'll see them fleeing the scene. Because of this song's repetitiveness, those children will stay, and may even try to hum or say the word, "Rock."

Toddlers learn through repetition. Children with difficulty paying attention need even more repetition. Play this game over and over throughout the day with several repetitions each time so that he "learns" the game.

As with all of our play routines, eventually your child should play this game several times in a row before moving on to another game or toy with you during your 1:1 play time.

Expand the Game:

1. Play with a new person. Have the other person watch you so they can play the game exactly like you do.

2. Play in a new place. After this routine is established, try it while she's sitting in the front of the grocery cart while you're waiting in line.

3. Alternate this play routine with "Up Down" or other ones that are on the floor to increase your child's ability to stay with you.

4. Proceed to the next set of activities, "Row Your Boat" and "Ride a Little Horsie," as more advanced versions of this game once you feel your child can tolerate more words.

ROW YOUR BOAT

<u>Materials</u>: None

<u>Great for a Child Who</u>:
Sits on your lap and holds your hands for at least a short time
Likes to be held, but really doesn't "connect" with you when you hold him
Likes to rock
Responds to music

<u>How to Play</u>:
Sit down on the floor with your legs outstretched in front of you and place your child on your legs facing you. Hold his hands and rock back and forward as you sing,

Row, row, row your boat,
Gently down the stream.
Merrily, merrily, merrily, merrily,
Life is but a dream.

Here's the fun second verse:

Row, row, row your boat,
Gently down the stream.
If you see an alligator,
> (Let go of your child's hands and make a big alligator mouth by opening and closing your outstretched arms and hands.)

Close your eyes and scream!
> (Cover your eyes for "close your eyes" and after you sing, "Scream," SCREAM!)

<u>Child's Goals</u>:
Of course the first goal is to have fun! Toddlers usually love this one! If her attention span is short and your child can't sit through the whole song, sing only the 2nd verse.

An initial goal for this game is to get him to stay through the entire song. If he tries to wiggle off your lap, try bouncing him on your legs while you sing. Try making the motions bigger with more energetic rowing and exaggerated words so he wants to stay for the scream at the end. For some children, you have to sing really, really FAST!

Encourage a real "scream" at the end of the song. Many non-verbal kids will imitate this when they can't yet imitate a word. Imitating a play sound like screaming is an important step toward imitating real words.

After you've played this one for a while, help him initiate this game with you by putting him on your lap, and then asking him if he wants to play, but not holding his hands to begin to row. Many kids initiate this with me by climbing on my lap, reaching down and grabbing both of my hands, and starting to rock back and forth. Sabotage this by leaving your hands in your lap, under your legs, or behind your back to get him to look for your hands, grab them, and begin the game.

Another goal is for her to perform the hand motions for the second verse. Help her do the motions after you've played this game many times. Once she's beginning to try to do the motions, let her complete those motions on her own with no help from you.

Young children learn through repetition. Toddlers with difficulty paying attention need even more repetition. Play this game over and over so that he "learns" the game.

As with all of our play routines, eventually your child should play this game several times in a row before moving on to another game or toy with you during your 1:1 play.

Expand the Game:
1. Play with a new person or in a new place. After this routine is established, try it while she's sitting in the front of the grocery cart or stroller while waiting.

2. Alternate this play routine with "Up Down" or other ones that are on the floor to increase your child's ability to stay with you.

3. Expand with new verses:
Row, row, row your boat,
Gently to the shore,
If you see a lion there,
Don't forget to roar!
      (ROAR loudly!)

Row, row, row your boat,
Down the Arctic river.
If you see a polar bear,
Don't forget to shiver.
      (Cross your arms and "shiver" like you're cold.)

RIDE A LITTLE HORSIE

<u>Materials</u>: None

<u>Great for a Child Who</u>:
Sits on your lap and holds your hands for at least a short time
Likes to be held, but really doesn't "connect" with you when you hold him
Likes to bounce and move
Likes "Up Down" or "Humpty Dumpty"
Responds to music

<u>How to Play</u>:
Here's another game for sitting on the floor with your child seated on your outstretched legs. Hold his hands; bounce him up and down on your legs, and sing or chant,

Ride a little horsie to town.
Watch out (child's name),
Don't.... fall..... down!
      (On down, spread your legs so that he falls through to the floor.)

When he's learning this one, pause and exaggerate, "Dooooon'tt...... faaall......" before you say, "Down," so he begins to anticipate the fall.

<u>Child's Goals</u>:
Of course the first goal is to participate and have fun! Toddlers love this one too!

An initial goal for this game is to get her to stay through the entire song. If she tries to wiggle off your lap, try bouncing her more vigorously (or sometimes, less vigorously).

After you've played this one for a while, help your child initiate this game with you by putting him on your lap and then asking him if he wants to play, but not offering your hands for him to hold right away. You want him to initiate this by reaching for your hands or bouncing up and down.

When a toddler has learned this game, I pause before I say, "Down," so that he will look down, smile or giggle, and perhaps even say, "Down" before I let him fall.

Young children learn through repetition. Toddlers with difficulty paying attention need even more repetition. Play this game over and over throughout the day with several repetitions each time so that he "learns" the game.

As with all of our play routines, eventually your child should play this game several times in a row before moving on to another game or toy with you during your 1:1 play time.

Expand the Game:

1. Play with a new person. Have the other person watch you so they can play the game exactly like you do.

2. Once a child likes this game and the previous one, "Row Your Boat," I alternate between these and have her choose which game she wants to play. You can ask, "Boat or horsie?" Rock a little when you say, "Boat," so she can respond with this gesture, and bounce her when you ask, "Horsie?" Look carefully for her action as to which one she might want. Or if your child seems to understand some simple yes/no questions, try nodding your head "yes" to see if she'll imitate that gesture as a way to answer your question when you ask, "Wanna ride horsie?" Responding to your question, in whatever way she can, is very communicative.

3. You might also introduce simple sign language for "more" as a way for your child to ask for additional turns. Ask him, "Want more?" As you're saying the word "more," sign "more" by closing your hands loosely and then bringing both hands to the middle in front of your body tapping your fingertips together several times. You can see this sign performed on my website at teachmetotalk.com. Click on the category Sign Language and check out the article, "Early Sign Vocabulary."

THIS IS THE WAY THE GENTLEMEN RIDE

<u>Materials</u>: None

<u>Great for a Child Who</u>:
Sits on your lap and holds your hands for at least a short time
Likes to be held, but really doesn't "connect" with you when you hold him
Likes to bounce and move
Likes "Up Down," "Humpty Dumpty," or "Ride a Little Horsie"
Responds to music

<u>How to Play</u>:
I'll just be honest and tell you that I NEVER sing this song like the original version. There are too many words to remember, and my version has also morphed into a "Wheels on the Bus" ending. Here's my version. Lightly bounce your child and sing,

This is the way the ladies ride,
The ladies ride, the ladies ride.
This is the way the ladies ride,
All through the town.

This is the way the gentlemen ride,
The gentlemen ride, the gentlemen ride.
This is the way the gentlemen ride,
All through the town.
    (Bounce your child a little bigger and sing a little louder on this verse.)

This is the way the cowboy rides,
The cowboy rides, the cowboy rides.
This is the way the cowboy rides.
All through the town.
    (Bounce much bigger and sing even louder and faster!)

This is the way the old man (or Grandpa) rides,
The old man rides, the old man rides.
This is the way the old man rides,
All through the town.
    (Bounce slowly and sing softly.)

This is the way (<u>child's name</u>) rides, (<u>name</u>) rides, (<u>name</u>) rides,
This is the way (<u>name</u>) rides,
All through the town.
>   (Pick your speed!)

Obviously you can use any name or kind of person here. I love how my friend and colleague Kate Hensler, a Developmental Interventionist, uses this game. She takes pictures of the child, mom, and dad, and then lets the child select the picture for who they will sing about next. This is a great idea for kids who don't yet say, "Mama" or "Dada" purposefully.

Child's Goals:

Your #1 goal is for your child to stay with you and have fun. You want to see him look at you, smile, and respond positively to you during the song. At first, he may stay only for a verse or two, but gradually increase this to see just how many different "people" he'll sit through.

Even verbal children who can repeat names of your family members will enjoy this game. Ask who you should sing about next giving choices such as, "Wanna ride like Mimi or Pappy?" A long-term goal would be for your child to independently tell you who comes next, but this may not happen for a while.

Young children learn through repetition. Toddlers with difficulty paying attention need even more repetition. Play this game over and over so that she "learns" the game.

As with all of our play routines, eventually your child should play this game several times in a row before moving on to another game or toy with you during your 1:1 play time.

Expand the Game:

1. Play the game with a new person. This is a new game, so you'll want to have the other person watch you so they play it the same way that you do.

2. This is a great game for anytime you're forced to sit and wait. You could do it holding your child on your lap, but you could also rock the stroller or grocery cart back and forth to simulate your speed for bouncing with the different verses.

3. If your child is fascinated with characters from a favorite TV show or movie, you could use those names for this song.

READY – SET – GO!

Materials: None

Great for a Child Who:
Has no or few other "games" he can play
Runs or walks randomly and is difficult to engage
Frequently ignores or avoids you
Has a very, very short attention span

How to Play:
When he's standing or running beside you, playfully catch him and say,

Ready....
> (Pull him close to you while you're saying the words.)

Set....
> (Continue holding him.)

Go!!!!
> (Let go and run with him across the room.)

I laugh and excitedly say, "Go, go, go, go, go!" as I run with a child. Try to run beside him or just in front of him as a way to entice him to look at you.

This is a great way to play WITH a child who likes to run with no regard for you.

Child's Goals:
Your first goal is for him to allow you to catch him and hold him while you say the words, "Ready...Set...Go!"

Your next goal is for him to run with you after you say, "Go!"

For a child who runs with no awareness that you're in the room, patiently initiate this game over and over until he "gets" it. Be persistent.

Next we want him laughing, smiling, and looking at you while you're running, and then watching you to see when you will catch him to begin the game again.

In the beginning you may need to say, "Ready, Set, Go!" quickly so that he doesn't have to wait too long to run. Over the next few days gradually increase the length of the wait to a few seconds between each word so that he begins to anticipate the word, "Go!"

After you've played this game for several days, build anticipation with your voice while you say, "Ready…Set….." and look at him expectantly to see if he will say, "Go!" on his own.

Young children learn through repetition. Toddlers with difficulty paying attention need even more repetition. Play this game over and over throughout the day with several repetitions each time so that he "learns" the game.

As with all of our play routines, eventually your child should play this game several times in a row before moving on to another game or toy with you during your 1:1 play time.

Expand the Game:

1. Play the game with a new person. Have the other person watch you play first so they can play the game exactly like you do.

2. This is a great game to play outside when you can't normally get your child's attention.

3. This game is a really fun way to begin to include Dad, siblings, one other little friend, or even to use with a small group of kids. Gross motor games, like running in a group, are often the first way we see children begin to interact with other friends their own age. This kind of activity happens well before toddlers begin to "play" cooperatively with other toys.

4. Another way you can advance the complexity of this game is for everyone to line up with their backs facing a wall and then wait to run until someone (or everyone) says, "Ready, Set, Go!" Run to the other side of the room, place your back against the wall, and begin this game again. I play this game when I see a child in a group or class at daycare or preschool.

5. If your child is playing with toys with you, you can generalize this phrase for races with cars, trains, or even when you're throwing or kicking balls.

GET 'CHA, GET 'CHA, GET 'CHA

Materials: None

Great for a Child Who:
Has no or few other "games" she can play
Runs or walks randomly and is difficult to engage
Frequently ignores or avoids you
Likes to be tickled
Loves roughhouse play or wrestling with you
Likes to be chased
Has a very, very short attention span

How to Play:
When your child is far enough away exaggerate big arm motions and take giant steps moving toward him slowly saying,

I'm......
Gonna......
>   (Build anticipation with your voice.)

Get 'cha, Get 'cha, Get 'cha!!   (Or "Get you! Get you! Get you!" if you prefer.)
>   (Run toward him and grab him! You can tickle him, pick him up and swing
>   him around, or even throw him, safely of course, down on the ground!)

Let him up, or put him down, and begin the game again. If he doesn't immediately try to run away from you to begin again, slowly walk backward while teasingly saying, "More? Want me to get you?" Begin again when you are far enough away to run toward him.

You may not want to initiate this game unless you can play for at least 10 minutes!

Child's Goals:
As with the previous games, participation is your initial goal. This is also a game where you can build longer "staying power" (Sonders, 2003) by increasing the amount of time your child *wants* to play WITH you, even if he doesn't initially know how to stay with you. For a child with a very short attention span, this is a great game because it's fast-paced, and it can be played even when he's not intending to play with you.

For a child who runs with no awareness that you're in the room, patiently initiate this game over and over until he "gets" it. Be persistent.

We want her to start to initiate this game by looking at you, even with just a small glance, as she turns to run away. Take advantage of this and chase her often in the beginning, even for several days or weeks, and then wait a few seconds before you begin to chase her to see if she'll give you an indication that she wants to be chased. Wait until she turns to look at you first before you begin, "I'm…. gonna…"

The best part of this game is helping a runner realize that it's fun to be caught!

Young children learn through repetition. Toddlers with difficulty paying attention need even more repetition. Play this game over and over throughout the day with several repetitions each time so that he "learns" the game.

As with all of our play routines, eventually your child should play this game several times in a row before moving on to another game or toy with you during your 1:1 play time.

Expand the Game:

1. Play with a new person. Have them watch you so they know exactly how to play.

2. Play in a new place. Try outside where he can really run.

3. Begin this play routine from a farther distance away, even from the other room. After she likes this routine and routinely indicates that she likes being caught, begin this routine when you're out of her sight. This trains her to look for you. Many children with social delays need help and motivation to learn to seek you out to play. Build this kind of opportunity for practice into your routines.

4. Try a longer version of this game recommended in the book Giggle Time by Susan Aud Sonders. Instead of "I'm Gonna Get 'Cha," she says,

Fee, Fie, Foe, Fum,
Big Giant, Here I come!

Fee, Fie, Foe, Fum,
Watch out, Here I come!

1-2-3 UP!   (or 1-2-3 JUMP!)

<u>Materials</u>: None

<u>Great for a Child Who:</u>
Has no or few other "games" she can play
Runs or walks randomly and is difficult to engage
Frequently ignores or avoids you
Likes to be lifted up in the air or jump
Has a very, very short attention span

<u>How to Play</u>:
While your child is standing on the floor (or in your lap for a child who's not standing alone), hold him under his arms counting,

One... Two.... Three.... UP!!

Lift her into the air on "Up." Jiggle her and laugh, and then lower her to your face to give her a kiss.

If a child is too heavy to lift over and over again, or if he prefers to jump, hold his hands while you're both standing and try this version:

One... Two.... Three.... JUMP!!

Then jump up and down with her while you're holding her hands.

If a child is not looking at me during this game, I get down on my knees so I'm face to face with him and bounce up and down as he jumps.

Don't forget to pause between the numbers and build excitement with your voice. Your child will likely soon want to repeat this game frequently, so be ready to play once you start!

Child's Goals:

As with the previous games, participation is the foremost goal. This is a game where you can also build longer "staying power" (Sonders, 2003) by repeating this game often and increasing the amount of time your child plays WITH you. For a child with a very short attention span, this is a great game because it's short, it's fast, and it's FUN!

After you've played this game for several days, pause before you say, "Up," or "Jump," to see if your child will initiate the action without you. Hopefully, you may even begin to hear the words "Up" or "Jump."

Pause between each number to see if your child will start to say, "Two," or "Three." Children often learn to count by rote if you routinely count to start your games.

Young children learn through repetition. Toddlers with difficulty paying attention need even more repetition. Play this game over and over throughout the day with several repetitions each time so that he "learns" the game.

As with all of our play routines, eventually your child should play this game several times in a row before moving on to another game or toy with you during your 1:1 play time.

Expand the Game:

1. Play with a new person.

2. Rotate between "Up" and "Jump."

3. Get a little creative and play in different ways. Let him jump off a chair or couch to you using the "1, 2, 3" cue. Or you can jump on the trampoline or the bed together. I bounce on my knees so that I'm eye level with a child.

4. This is also an activity you can try when you're holding your child's hands while waiting in line. Your child can get the movement he needs, yet stay in one place with you.

1-2-3 FLY!

<u>Materials</u>: A soft surface such as a bed, the couch, or a big, comfortable chair

<u>Great for a Child Who</u>:
Has no or few other "games" he can play
Runs or walks randomly and is difficult to engage
Frequently ignores or avoids you
Likes to swing or be lifted up in the air
Likes to crash into objects or fall down
Has a very, very short attention span

<u>How to Play</u>:
When you're both standing in front of the bed, ask your child,

Wanna fly?
> (Pick your child up with one hand on his chest and the other hand on his stomach from behind.)

1....2....3....
> (Swing your child forward toward the surface on each number.)

FLY!
> (Gently toss your child onto the bed. Sometimes I say, "Boom" when the child lands on the bed, or "Whee" instead of "Fly" if I think the child might imitate these words.)

<u>Child's Goals</u>:
The first goal is for your child to allow you to lift her off the floor. Of course you want her to respond positively and connect with you by sustaining eye contact, smiling, and laughing.

Next we want him to come toward you when you hold out your hands and call him over to play, either by calling his name, or by asking, "Fly?" Wait for him to come to you before you pick him up to play. If he doesn't come over, keep asking him, "Fly? Wanna fly?" Pick him up and begin again.

The next goal is for him to lift up his arms to be picked up to begin the game. Stand in front of him and wiggle your fingers as an invitation for him to reach for your hands to be picked up. Don't pick him up until he lifts up his arms. If he doesn't, bend down a little and lean closer to encourage him to do some of the work too!

If he starts to run away, then scoop him up and begin to play this game again.

Young children learn through repetition. Toddlers with difficulty paying attention need even more repetition. Play this game over and over throughout the day for several repetitions each time so that he "learns" the game.

As with all of our play routines, eventually your child should play this game several times in a row before moving on to another game or toy with you during your 1:1 play time.

Expand the Game:

1. Play the game with a new person. Have the other person watch you so they can play the game the same way that you do.

2. Play in a new place. Try grandma's house or a friend's home. Try outside on the trampoline.

 3. Try to alternate this game with 1-2-3 Up/Jump, but most kids prefer the flying game!

ROCKET SHIP

<u>Materials</u>: None

<u>Great for a Child Who</u>:
Has no or few other "games" he can play
Frequently ignores or avoids you
Likes to swing or be lifted up in the air
Has a very, very short attention span
Seeks pressure on his stomach

<u>How to Play</u>:
Lie down on the floor on your back with your feet on the floor and your knees up. Ask your child, "Rockets? Play rockets?" When he seems to want to play, say,

Rockets!!
> (Hold your child under his arms and place him on the front of your legs with his chest on your knees and shins.)

3 – 2 – 1.....
> (Gently rock your child on your legs as you countdown.)

Blast off!!
> (Lift your feet off the ground and bring your knees to your chest. Move him around like that for a few seconds and say, "Whee!" or "Fly!")

Down!
> (Lower your child to the ground and begin again.)

Some parents call this game, "Superman" or "Superbaby."

<u>Child's Goals:</u>
The first goal is for your child to allow you to lift him off the floor. Of course, you want him to respond positively and connect with you by sustaining eye contact, smiling, and laughing.

Next we want him to come toward you when you lie down on the floor and call him over to play, either by calling his name, or by asking, "Rockets? Wanna play rockets?"

Wait for him to lean on your legs before you lift him up. We want this to be his way to participate and respond to begin the game.

After you've played for a while, you may leave your legs flat on the floor, and see if he will push your knees up. When he does this, ask, "Up? Up? My knees up?"

Model the same word, "Whee," or "Fly," every time you play this game to see if your child will start to say this too, but some kids can only laugh while in this position!

If she's beginning to try to count, you may want to alter the countdown and say, "1, 2, 3," instead so she can try to count with you.

Young children learn through repetition. Toddlers with difficulty paying attention need even more repetition. Play this game over and over throughout the day with several repetitions each time so that he "learns" the game.

As with all of our play routines, eventually your child should play this game several times in a row before moving on to another game or toy with you during your 1:1 play time.

Expand the Game:
1. Play the game with a new person. Have the other person watch you first so they can play it the same way you do.

2. Play on a bed if you have a bad back!

MARCHING, MARCHING

<u>Materials</u>: None

<u>Great for a Child Who:</u>
Runs or walks around randomly
Marches, jumps, or stomps often
Likes music and attends to singing

<u>How to Play</u>:
When your child is walking around the room, get in front of him and sing to the tune of "Are you Sleeping" or "Frere Jacques,"

Marching, Marching,
Marching, Marching,
Hop, Hop, Hop,
Hop, Hop, Hop,
Running, Running, Running,
Running, Running, Running,
Now we stop!

Perform the appropriate actions as you sing the words. Make each action BIG so he doesn't miss the changes that accompany your words. On "Stop," make a big deal about stopping dead in your tracks, and slap your hands down on your legs. This teaches him to associate "stop" with no movement of his arms or legs, which is *really* stopping! This is something you want him to hear and understand that he should do when you say, "Stop!"

After a moment, begin to clap and say, "Yay!" Then begin the song again.

Another version of this song is to sing, "Walking, Walking," rather than, "Marching, Marching," but I prefer the bigger action of marching. However, if your child frequently runs away from you, you may prefer to teach, "WALK!" Sing this version of the song to help him differentiate between those two verbs!

Child's Goals:

The first goal is for your child to pay attention to what you're doing and watch your movements as you sing the song.

Next we want her to try to imitate those actions. Children usually understand the "running" part first! If she's not running or hopping on the appropriate part, get behind her and hold her under her arms to help her run or lift her up under her arms to hop. You should also help her "stop" by catching her if she continues to run and help her slap her hands on her own legs.

Watch for your child to initiate this game with "marching" at different times around the house, or if you see him taking big steps, begin to sing the song to encourage him to play and initiate the game on his own.

This is a fun way to help focus a child's need to walk or run as you're trying to play with him and he prefers to run around. Moving is part of the game!

It's a great way to get his attention when he's running and ignoring you after he's learned the game. When he's trying to run away from you, loudly march and sing, "Marching, Marching…"

Young children learn through repetition. Toddlers with difficulty paying attention need even more repetition. Play this game over and over throughout the day with several repetitions each time so that he "learns" the game.

As with all of our play routines, eventually your child should play this game several times in a row before moving on to another game or toy with you during your 1:1 play time.

Expand the Game:

1. Introduce new people so that he can hear others sing and see others doing the correct actions in the song.

2. Use this as a transition activity while you're moving to another part of your home to start a new daily routine. One family uses this as a way to move to the bathroom for a bath and the dining room to eat.

3. Introduce the next activity, "Ring Around the Rosies," if your child likes this game.

RING AROUND THE ROSIES

Materials: None

Great for a Child Who:
Runs or walks around randomly
Marches, jumps, or stomps around often
Likes music and attends to singing
Likes to crash into objects or fall down
Is beginning to be interested in watching other children
Likes to hold your hands to lead you to what he wants
Has an older sibling who will play this game over and over again!

How to Play:
When your child is standing, grab his hands and say, "Play Rosies!"

I like to start this game by bending my knees on each word and saying, "Ready...Set ... Go!" to build anticipation. Then walk in a circle holding hands as you sing,

Ring around the rosies.
Pocket full of posies.
Ashes, ashes.
We all.....
Fall.....
Down.
　　　(Fall to the floor on "down.")

Clap and say, "Yay!"

Get up and repeat the entire game several times.

If a child doesn't look up at my face while we're playing, I get down on my knees to play, so that I'm eye level with him.

For kids who won't hold my hands to walk around in a circle, I stand up and hold them while I turn in a circle and sing. On "Down," I gently drop them to the floor.

Child's Goals:
Participation for the entire game is the initial goal. Some children will want to fall down

sooner than you should, so keep singing and drag them along until the end. For those kids, sing faster!

This is a great game for kids who need to move, even while they play with you. Movement is part of the game. Walk faster or even jump around in a circle for extra "oomph" to help that kind of child stay with you.

For some children who don't like being touched, just holding another person's hands for the entire song is success!

After you've played for a while and your child knows this game, pause after you say, "Ready... Set..." and wait for your child to say, "Go."

When you've played for several days, pause and look expectantly at your child before saying, "Down," to see if he'll say, "Down," on his own.

Young children learn through repetition. Toddlers with difficulty paying attention need even more repetition. Play this game over and over throughout the day with several repetitions each time so that he "learns" the game.

As with all of our play routines, eventually your child should play this game several times in a row before moving on to another game or toy with you during your 1:1 play time.

Expand the Game:

1. This game is a fantastic way to introduce other people into your play routines, whether it be Dad, an older sibling, or a little friend. Start the game 1:1 with you for at least a few turns, or even several days, so that he learns the routine, and then add other people. If he's reluctant to hold another child's hand, play with another adult or an older child who will grab and hold onto his hand for the entire game.

2. Expand the game by staying on the floor until your child pulls you up for another round. To help him learn to do this, offer your hands to see if he will grab them and pull you up. Ask, "More? Up?" so that he'll learn to use these words to get you to play again. If he doesn't try to pull you up, have another person pull you up, so he can see the effects of that action.

3. Sometimes this game is a great way to redirect a child who gets stuck wanting to lead you around with no real goal or intent.

NIGHT-NIGHT GAME

Materials: None

Great for a Child Who:
Frequently lies on the floor
Is just beginning to understand early pretend games (but this is not required!)

How to Play:
I usually initiate this game when a child is lying down on the floor. Get down on the floor right in front of him and say,

Night-night?

Night-night!
>   (Loudly yawn and pat your mouth, stretch your arms out and over your head, then place your hands together on one side of your face. Lie or crouch down on the floor face-to-face with your child.)

Shhhhh!
>   (Place your index finger in front of your mouth while saying, "Shhh!")

Night-night!
>   (Close your eyes and exaggerate several snores. After a few seconds, open your eyes and whisper,)

1, 2, 3......
>   (Hold up your fingers as you count.)

WAKE UP!
>   (Yell this loudly as you suddenly sit up. I usually continue to yell, "Ahh" as I wave my arms around and act as silly as I can.)

I also play while I'm sitting on the floor and place my head on a couch or chair to "sleep."

Child's Goals:

As with all your games, we initially want to watch for his responses. At first he may just watch you do this whole routine while he continues to lie there. We do want him to like this game after a few times of watching you play alone. Of course we want him to connect with you by looking at you, smiling, and laughing.

Help him lie down for "Night-night" and sit up when you say, "Wake up!" if he doesn't do this on his own.

This is a good game to elicit vocalization attempts and imitation. Your child can yell with you at the end of the game, say, "Shhhh," and "snore" when you're pretending to sleep.

If your child tries to count in other games, pause after you say, "1," to see if he'll say, "2, 3," as you hold up your fingers. You may trying mouthing the words to see if he'll say them.

Young children learn through repetition. Toddlers with difficulty paying attention need even more repetition. Play this game over and over throughout the day with several repetitions each time so that he "learns" the game.

As with all of our play routines, eventually your child should play this game several times in a row before moving on to another game or toy with you during your 1:1 play time.

Expand the Game:

1. Play the game with a new person. Have the other person watch you so they can play the game the same way that you do.

2. You can incorporate some early pretend play into this game with dolls or stuffed animals by having them play the game too. Pat the baby doll as you say, "Night-night." Then continue with your whole routine making the doll jump up as you say, "Wake up!"

3. Watch for your child to initiate this game when he hears you say, "Night-night," during play or anytime he's on the floor.

(Many parents tell me that they have made the mistake of playing this game at bedtime, and then it takes a long time for their child to settle down to go to sleep. Save this routine for during the day when it's clearly a game!)

MOMMY AND BABY ELEPHANTS

<u>Materials</u>: None

<u>Great for a Child Who</u>:
Runs or walks around randomly
Likes to crash into objects or fall down
Likes to roughhouse
Likes to swing
Seeks pressure on his stomach

<u>How to Play</u>:
When you are across the room from your child say,

Here comes Mommy Elephant.
> (Do the sign for elephant. I use a baby signs version which is lifting up one arm like it's an elephant raising its trunk. Make an elephant sound.)

Here comes Mommy Elephant. Here comes Mommy Elephant.
> (Chant this several times as you move across the room like an elephant. Bend down from your waist, join both hands together, and swing your arms from side to side, as you stomp across the room. About half way to reaching your child stand up, look around, and then begin to chant,)

Where's my Baby Elephant? Where's my Baby Elephant?

There's my Baby Elephant!
> (Point at your child, and then swing your arms like before and stomp over to get her.)

Baby Elephant, want a ride/up?
> (Pick up your child from behind, clasping your hands and putting them on her belly, and then pick her up with your hands under her belly. Swing her as you stomp across the room. Say something like, "Whoa!" or "Whee!" as you swing your child.)

Baby Elephant - All done! (or "Down.")
> (Then drop your child to the floor.)

Clap and cheer saying, "Yay!"

Repeat the game by walking away from your child, then turning around to start over.

Child's Goals:

As with all of our games, your #1 goal is for your child to love this so much he wants to play over and over again.

You want him to stay with you and anticipate you picking him up, so make the time it takes for you to get to him and pick him up very short at first. As he begins to understand and love the game, begin further away from him so that he gets excited and anticipates you picking him up.

For responses, you can expect your child to move toward you and into your hands to be picked up. "Twinkly" eyes and a giggle are good responses initially, even if she doesn't move into your hands.

After you've played this game for a while, if your child can nod or say yes, or can repeat the words "up" or "ride," wait until he says that word before picking him up.

You could try to elicit the sign or word "more" to begin the game again, but play again anyway if you ask your child 2 or 3 times and get no response other than a look that tells you, "YES!"

Young children learn through repetition. Toddlers with difficulty paying attention need even more repetition. Play this game over and over throughout the day with a few repetitions each time so that he "learns" the game.

As with all of our play routines, eventually your child should play this game several times in a row before moving on to another game or toy with you during your 1:1 play time.

Expand the Game:

1. Play the game with a new person. Have the other person watch you several times so they play it the same way that you do.

2. Add new animals. You could be a bear, a horsie, or any other animal your child likes. Instead of picking your child up, try giving him a ride on your back. Rather than being carried under their bellies, some kids like to stand on your foot and hang onto your leg while you stomp across the room. I call this version, "Baby Monkeys."

3. Once this play routine is well-established, initiate it from another room. Or use this as a way to call your child to come to you when he's ignoring you. Play the game for a few minutes, and then since you have his attention, you can move on to the real reason you called him. Children will often happily approach you if they think there's something fun in it for them. Use this to your advantage! Play one of your little games first so that he learns to eagerly respond to your calls, and then move on to your next order of business with him.

Early Toys

Before you run out and buy the toys listed here, remember that no toy can substitute for an engaged, nurturing, responsive, and FUN parent as a play partner! The **main** reason any of these activities will be successful for you is because you'll be <u>PLAYING</u> <u>WITH</u> your child. Don't offer the toy and sit by watching and waiting for him to play. Show him how to play, and most of all, play WITH him.

I also want to take a minute to interject what kinds of toys a child with social and language delays should not have at home. On my website at teachmetotalk.com I wrote an article titled, "Ditch the Bells, Whistles, Flashing Lights, DVDs and ABCs!" This has become my mantra to parents of children with social delays. These kinds of electronic, musical and alphabet toys actually prohibit social skill development in many children. Toy manufacturers have spent millions of dollars to trick parents into thinking that these toys are "educational" since they include early academic concepts. What good is it if a child knows his letters, numbers, colors, and shapes, but can't ask for milk or respond when his mom calls his name?

Some children become so engrossed in sensory-seeking behaviors with light and sound toys that they miss out on the fun and benefits of more typical play. All a child like this wants to do is push buttons to the exclusion of interaction with real people or more challenging toys. If your child is already hooked on these kinds of toys, let the batteries run down and don't replace them. Sometimes parents don't like to hear this advice. They struggle with taking away what their child seems to love. It's up to you, but if you want your child to learn to be more engaged with others, I'd get rid of those kinds of toys today, or at least put them on the top shelf of the closet.

Many parents also allow children with social delays to watch children's television programs or DVDs and think of this as "educational" time. Cutting-edge research in brain development tells us that quickly changing visual stimuli seen in children's programming or in TV commercials may actually wire a child's developing brain to "scan and shift." In her book, <u>Bright From the Start,</u> neuroscientist Jill Stamm hypothesizes that habitual television and video viewing for infants and toddlers may be the reason for the surge in childhood ADD in our country. Many leading experts, including the American Academy of Pediatrics, recommend no "screen time" including television, DVDs, or computer games, for children under 2 and very limited viewing during the toddler and preschool years. Dr. Stanley Greenspan, America's leading authority on treating autism in children, advocates no television viewing for children with, or who are suspected to be at risk for, autism. This guideline is difficult for many families to implement, but in my own practice I have seen so many young children make huge gains in their ability to interact with others, play with toys, and begin to use words when their parents eliminated TV and videos on a daily basis.

Now for what you can and should do....

The following activities are the same ones I use during speech therapy sessions with young children who aren't very interested in toys yet. Most of these games are with toys you probably have at home. Some aren't "toys" at all, but household items you likely already own. These are my go-to-games when I need to get a kid's attention in the beginning sessions when he's not "with" me yet. Even later during the therapy process I use these games when I feel like I am losing the child's focus and attention, especially between sit-down play with more traditional toys. I believe that ALL of us need to move, especially when we're learning something brand new like interacting and talking, so that we stay alert, regulated, and focused. A lethargic, inattentive, BORED child is not in an optimal state for interacting or communicating, so GET UP, MOVE, and PLAY!

Start with these routines if your child has limited interest in playing WITH you with toys. Each of the following activities initially requires little or no participation on your child's part, other than he pause his activity to look at you. As you play the game more and more, we want to expand his attention into a true social reaction so that he maintains eye contact, smiles, and even laughs as he watches you play the game. Next you'll help him begin to participate in the game and learn to truly play WITH you. Finally, we want him to engage you in play as he initiates the game he now loves!

On each page you'll find:

- The name of the game
- Materials required
- Description of a child's preferences to help you decide if this game is a good match for your child
- Detailed instructions in "How to Play" including what key words and sounds YOU should say when playing
- List of child's goals so that you'll know what responses to shoot for, how to help your child move to a more advanced response, and how to measure progress
- Problem solving tips specific to each game
- Ideas for expanding the game and new games to try when he's mastered the first one

If your child doesn't seem to enjoy a particular toy or activity on your first few attempts, don't give up! Keep at it. Repetition builds familiarity, and once a child recognizes the game, he's more likely to want to play with the toy and you.

During my initial sessions with children with social and language delays, I alternate between playing the kinds of social games listed in the previous chapter and using play with these simple toys. When I feel like a child's attention is waning, I move back and forth between easy social games and early toys so that I am always "recapturing" his interest.

At the end of this section, you'll find a list of other toys I like and use in speech therapy sessions.

Let me remind you again that what YOU say during these games is important. I've included the same key words and play sounds I use when I play these games during speech therapy. Don't forget that exclamatory words and play sounds are often easier for a child who tunes out speech to attend to and then try to imitate. Check the list from the last chapter to refresh your memory. Most of these words are easy to pronounce too, so they give a child a better shot at success when you're working to get those first word attempts.

Don't forget my other advice about the language you use. Keep your words simple, and speak only in single words and short 2-3 word phrases. Use a sing-song or melodic voice to capture your child's attention. Repeat your key words and phrases over and over. Don't be so afraid of saying the wrong thing that you're too quiet, but make sure what you do say are words that your child can understand, and in time, will be able to repeat.

One last word of advice, get ready to play! Turn off your phone and the TV. Ignore any other distractions. As in the previous section, your goal is for your child to want to play with you for at least 10 minutes, and hopefully, even longer.

Remember that the toy you're using isn't nearly as important as interacting with your child. Be flexible. Be creative. If something I've suggested isn't working, come up with your own new twist.

Plaster a huge smile on your face, and get ready to woo your baby into interacting with you as you play. She's waiting…

BALLS

Materials:
Start with any ball your child likes. My favorites with older toddlers and young preschoolers are the very small rubber "bouncy" balls, but don't get them so small that your young child could swallow them. Ping pong balls are also entertaining.

Great for a Child Who:
Isn't that interested in regular toys yet
Likes to look at things that spin or move
Likes to hold small objects in his hands

How to Play:
For kids who are really visual, play in a larger, uncarpeted space away from any breakable items. Hold the ball so that your child can see it and eagerly say, "BALL!" Bounce your ball as high as you can. Say, "Wow," "Wheeeeee," or even squeal as the ball bounces.

This will be a real attention-getter for your child since you probably haven't played in this way before. Using vocalizations that aren't real words is a great way to get a child who normally tunes out speech to attend to you. Try other silly words as the ball bounces such as "boop" or any other sound that seems to mimic the way your ball sounds as it bounces on the floor. After several bounces, make a big deal about catching the ball. Say, "BALL!" or "Got it!" as you excitedly grab the ball and begin again. Repeat your same sequence of play being careful not to add too many extra words. Too many extra new words may overload your child, and he may shut down and walk away.

If your child grabs the ball and wants to bounce it himself, GREAT! Use the same words you used when you bounced the ball, "BALL! - WHEE!! - Got it!" On the next turn, beat him to the ball and grab it yourself! Laugh, smile, and be animated and very playful as you grab the ball to make sure he understands this is a game and that you're not trying to take the ball from him. Immediately bounce the ball again so that he gets a turn to catch and bounce it himself. If he doesn't try to catch the ball and bounce it himself, you're probably not being fun enough. Try again, and bounce the ball right in front of him being even more excited and playful. If he doesn't get the ball and bounce it himself after a few more tries, hold the ball out to him as his invitation to try, and ask, "Ball? Your turn?"

If your child routinely grabs the ball and runs rather than bouncing it, or gets too upset when you have a turn, try using two balls so that he can hold one, but continue to do everything you can to engage him. If he turns his back on you, run around in front of him and bounce your ball. You might try to grab his ball too if he's not interested in you, but make it so playful that he knows you're joking. Bounce the ball quickly so he has a chance to retrieve his ball before he's too upset.

If he's just sitting or standing there, or worse, walking away, try other ways to pull him into play with the ball. Balance the ball on your head, or roll it down his arm. Hide the ball in his pocket or under his shirt. Animatedly ask, "Where's ball?" Look under him, behind him, or in his ear asking, "Where's ball? Is it here?" Say, "Noooo!" each time you don't find it. Build anticipation with your voice each time you look in a new spot. After 3 or 4 wrong places, find the ball and say, "There's ball! Got it!" After a good laugh, stand up and begin your bouncing routine again "wooing" him to play *with* you.

Child's Goals:

Of course our #1 goal is for your child to join you in play by taking turns with you bouncing and chasing the ball. Look for his reactions. He should be giggling and have those "twinkly" eyes as you each bounce and catch the ball.

If he's not smiling, laughing, and having a great time, then chances are you're not being fun enough. As I tell every parent and therapist I work with, "Ratchet it up a notch!" He's got to believe that YOU are having a blast.

Secondary goals would be for him to begin to imitate the simple, repetitive sounds and key words you've been using. Be sure you're not using too many different words during this play routine so that he can pick out which words to imitate.

If he's not joining in play yet, but he's beginning to watch you more, keep trying! If you are fun enough, simple enough, and repetitive enough, he will join you in play.

We want your child to play this game with you for 10 minutes or longer.

Expand the Game

1. Slowly add a new person to your game. Coach the person ahead of time not to add too many new words or vary the game so much that you lose your child's participation and interest. If your child begins to walk away or have a meltdown, you've probably changed the game too much for him right now.

Sometimes a child can handle an adult or a much older child joining in the game, but not a child near his own age. In the beginning adding a sibling, especially one that's very close in age, creates so much jealousy and stress that your child can't continue to play. In that case save this game for 1:1 playtime with you or have another adult join you.

2. I also love Phlat balls which can be purchased at most major retailers such as Walmart or Target. You can usually find these balls on the aisle with the Nerf toys. These are balls you push "flat," and after a few seconds, the ball pops back out to its normal size. The popping surprise is an instant attention-getter and usually elicits a reaction from a child. Toddlers need help to learn to push the ball flat, and their little fingers can get caught in the edges, so save this toy for play with an adult. The directions suggest throwing the Phlat ball so it will pop open in the air, but I use it on the floor for toddlers. It's a great toy for sensory-seekers and for kids who crave deep pressure. I also use it for turn-taking practice since the turns are fast and fun, even if you're not the one who gets to push the ball. Create your play routine using words like "Push," saying, "Wait - wait - wait" until the ball opens, and then say, "POP!" Take turns pushing the ball flat. I pat my legs each time I say, "Wait-wait!" The child learns not to reach for the ball until it pops open, and we're ready for another turn.
3. If you have a large space or are outside, try beach balls or soccer balls for this play routine. Beach balls are light enough for most toddlers to throw and carry. The black and white visual pattern soccer balls create when they roll is very stimulating and enticing for some children.

4. Many therapists will encourage you to try to get your child to roll the ball back and forth with you as a form of "social" play. This might be fun for children who can't walk yet, but for the rest of them, it's usually B-O-R-I-N-G. I prefer bouncing, throwing, and kicking over rolling, and most young children do too!

5. Make this kind of play even more social by asking for a turn. After your child has had several turns with the ball, hold your hand out and say, "Give me the ball," or "My turn?" If he doesn't give you the ball after several attempts, keep your hand open, and then use your other hand to "help" him place the ball in your open hand. Bounce or throw the ball quickly to keep your child interested in playing the game with you.

6. Your child might enjoy using a basket, an open box, or even a child-size basketball goal. Expand the game so that you're adding this new step of throwing the ball into a container while keeping him playing WITH you.

WIND UP TOYS

Materials:
Any small toy that must be wound up before it will move usually requires help from an adult. Most of these toys are animals or vehicles that walk, jump, or roll after winding. These toys are popular around holidays like Christmas and Easter in major retailers.

Great for a Child Who:
Isn't that interested in regular toys yet
Likes to look at things that spin or move

How to Play:
When your child is near you, wind up the toy, and place it on the table or floor so that your child can see it move. While you're winding it, say something like, "Ooooh! Look!" Say, "Wow!" as the toy moves. Act excited by clapping or saying, "Yay!" when it's finished. Expectantly look at your child and ask, "More?" Wind it up and begin again.

When your child reaches for the toy to examine it or tries to wind it up on his own, hold out your hand and ask, "Want help?" Repeat this several times to encourage him to give you the toy for assistance, but don't let him walk away, or he may lose interest. If he doesn't give you the toy after a few tries, have another person help him place it in your hand, or use your free hand to help him place the toy in your open hand. As soon as you get the toy, wind it up, and begin again to hold his attention. If he doesn't look at you at all, hold the toy close to your face while you wind it and ask, "More?"

If your child doesn't come over to watch, make a bigger deal about the toy.

If he's not attending at all, wait until later and try again when he's seated in his high chair or at a table and is less apt to walk away.

Child's Goals:
Of course our #1 goal is for your child to participate by watching the toy move and wanting to see it again and again. Look for his reactions. He should be giggling and watching the toy. If he's not smiling, laughing, and having a great time, then chances are, you're not being fun enough. As I tell every parent and therapist I work with, "Ratchet it up a notch!" He's got to believe you're having FUN playing *with* him.

BUBBLES

Materials:
You can use any container of bubbles, but no-spill bubble containers changed my life! I love the smaller ones with characters on the wands that kids recognize. You can find those at major retailers when the stores add the spring and summer toys at the beginning of the season. I do not use automatic bubble blowers since I want kids to try to blow bubbles too. Imitating blowing is a <u>great</u> way to get toddlers to start to imitate any kind of mouth movement.

Great for a Child Who:
Isn't that interested in regular toys yet
Likes to look at things that spin or move
Doesn't make eye contact regularly since he will notice your face more as you blow

How to Play:
Sit on the floor with the container. Say, "BUBBLES!" Blow bubbles using exaggerated facial expressions. Exclaim, "BUBBLES!" or other play sounds like "Oooo," or "WOW!" When the bubbles reach the ground, use your whole hand to slap the bubble and loudly say, "POP!" This is a real attention-getter and often encourages your child to imitate the action you're doing, smacking the floor with your hand. This is often the very first "participation" I get in play with a child. If your child is popping bubbles in mid-air with his fingers, say, "POP!" You can also catch bubbles with your wand and hold the wand toward your child so that she can see the bubble and then pop it with her finger. Take her hand and help her if she can't pop the bubble on her own if your physical assistance doesn't make her too mad.

If your child begins to look around for more bubbles, say, "All gone. More? Bubbles?" If you're using words or signs like, "more" or "please" to request an additional turn, prompt this here, but for a child who is *very* difficult to engage, play without any demands for a response other than your child stay with you to play bubbles. If this is the case, ask, "More?" or "Bubbles?" then immediately launch into another turn without requiring the verbal or signed response just yet.

Hold the wand in front of your child's mouth and give her a chance to blow. Say, "Blow!" Many children end up putting the wand in their mouths instead of blowing, so try to curb this by holding the wand yourself. Show your child how to blow. If your child wants to hold the bubbles, try giving him his own wand, or possibly give him his own small, spill-proof bubble container to hold, but be careful with this. Sometimes giving a child his own container eliminates the need to include you in his play, and that's the whole point of this game!

Child's Goals:

Of course our #1 goal is for your child to participate by watching and popping the bubbles. Look for his reactions. He should be giggling and have those "twinkly" eyes as you each blow and pop bubbles. We also want him to look at you, so make yourself very fun to watch as you blow the bubbles. Exaggerate animated and silly facial expressions. Make your cheeks big and widen your eyes as you blow.

If he's not smiling, laughing, and having a great time, then chances are, you are not being fun enough. As I tell every parent and therapist I work with, "Ratchet it up a notch!" He's got to believe you're having FUN playing *with* him.

Secondary goals would be for him to imitate the simple, repetitive sounds and key words you've been saying. Be sure you're not using too many different words.

If he's not joining in by popping bubbles, but is watching the bubbles and you more, keep trying! If you are fun enough, simple enough, and repetitive enough, he will join you.

As with all of our play routines, we want your child to play this game for 10 minutes or longer.

Expand the Game

1. Slowly add a new person to your game. Coach the person ahead of time not to add too many new words or vary the game so much that you lose your child's participation and interest. If your child begins to walk away or have a meltdown, you've probably changed the game too much for him right now. Sometimes a child can handle an adult or a much older child joining in the game, but not a child near his own age. In the beginning adding a sibling, especially one that's very close in age, creates too much jealousy and stress so that your child can't continue to play. In that case, save this game for 1:1 playtime with you or with another adult.

2. Try bubbles in a new place such as the bathtub or outside.

3. If you're using those mechanical blowers that are activated with a button, be sure to keep the game social by making sure that you're still included. Maintain control of the blower so that you still have a role.

BALLOONS

Materials:
Package of balloons

Great for a Child Who:
Isn't that interested in regular toys yet
Likes to look at things that spin or move
Doesn't make eye contact regularly since he will notice your face more as you blow

How to Play:
Hold one balloon close to your face and excitedly say, "Balloon!" Begin to blow using exaggerated facial expressions. Make your face fun for her to watch. I widen my eyes, puff out my cheeks, and raise my eyebrows as I blow. I also say, "Blow!" between breaths.

When the balloon is big enough, tie the end and say, "WOW!!! Balloon!" Throw the balloon in the air and say, "Uuuuuup" or "Wheeeeee!" Hit the balloon into the air with your hands. Say other play sounds like, "Whoa," when you're reaching for the balloon as it falls to the ground, or "Oooooh!" Using a vocalization that's not a real word is often a great way to get a child's attention who normally tunes out speech.

Some children will try to grab the balloon and sit or lie down on it. Some kids will try to put their mouths on the end to blow it up again. That's okay since he's participating with you. Follow your child's lead, and continue to use your same key words. For example, if he's placed the balloon on the floor and then gets on top of it, say "Balloon got your belly!" If he's not including you in this play, quickly grab the balloon and throw it in the air to begin your routine again. Keep it fun and playful so that he doesn't get too mad, but make sure you're included in the game.

Child's Goals:
Like our previous activities, our #1 goal is for your child to participate by playing with the balloon. Look for her reactions. She should be laughing, smiling, and have those "twinkly" eyes as you throw, catch, chase, and hit the balloon.

If he's not smiling, laughing, and having a great time, then chances are you're not being fun enough. As I tell every parent and therapist I work with, "Ratchet it up a notch!" He's got to believe you're having FUN playing *with* him.

Secondary goals would be for her to imitate the simple, repetitive sounds and key words you've been saying. Be sure you're not using too many different words during this play routine.

If she's not joining in, but even beginning to watch the balloon and you more, keep trying! If you are fun enough, simple enough, and repetitive enough, she will join you in play.

As with all of our play routines, we want your child to play this game for 10 minutes or longer.

Expand the Game

1. Slowly add a new person to your game. Coach the person ahead of time not to add too many new words or vary the game so much that you lose your child's participation and interest. If your child begins to walk away or have a meltdown, you've probably changed the game too much for her right now. Sometimes a child can handle an adult or a much older child joining in the game, but not a child near her own age. In the beginning adding a sibling, especially one that's very close in age, creates too much jealousy so that your child can't continue to play. In that case save this game for 1:1 playtime with you or with another adult.

2. Instead of tying the balloon after you've blown it up, let go so that the balloon flies around the room. Young children either love this, or they're scared to death. If your child hates loud noises, this may be too over-stimulating for him.

3. Make this kind of play even more social by asking for a turn. When your child has had several turns with the balloon, hold your hands out and say, "Give me balloon," or "My turn?" If he's not giving you the balloon after several attempts, keep one hand open, and then use your other hand to "help" him place the balloon in your open hand. Quickly throw the balloon again so he doesn't feel like you're taking the balloon away from him. If this makes him too mad, then just continue to play and save this "sharing" step for a couple of days or weeks. In the beginning the most important thing is that he continues to enjoy playing *with* you.

FOLLOW ME

Materials:

Use your child's favorite stuffed animal or doll for this game. You can even try a smaller toy like Thomas the train if that's the only toy your child likes.

Great for a Child Who:

Has one favorite toy

Likes to look at things that spin or move

Likes to hold small objects in his hands

How to Play:

Tie a long piece of string (6-8 feet) around the toy. Some kids like it if the end is in another room and they can't see you pulling the string.

Put the toy in the middle of the room. Call the toy using its name (ie: Elmo, baby, Thomas, etc...) Then say, "Come here" or "Come on" or whatever phrase you say to your child to call him to come to you.

Pull the string to make the toy move. If your child doesn't follow the toy, have Dad or another adult "coach" your child and say things like, "There goes ___," "Go get ___," or "Let's go!" The person should demonstrate how to chase and catch the toy.

When your child "catches" the toy, you should say the toy's name or "Got it!"

Play again!

Child's Goals:

Like our previous activities, our #1 goal is for your child to participate by trying to follow and catch the toy. Look for his reactions. He should be laughing, smiling, and have those "twinkly" eyes as you chase and catch the toy.

If he's not smiling, laughing, and having a great time, then chances are you're not being fun enough. As I tell every parent and therapist I work with, "Ratchet it up a notch!" He's got to believe you're having FUN playing *with* him.

Secondary goals would be for him to imitate the simple, repetitive sounds and key words you've been saying. Be sure you're not using too many different words during this play routine.

If he's not joining in, but even beginning to watch the toy and you more, keep trying! If you are fun enough, simple enough, and repetitive enough, he will join you in play.

If your child doesn't understand how to play this game by catching the toy, have another adult or an older child play this several times to demonstrate how to play. Then the other person can "help" your child follow along by getting behind him or her and gently nudging him to encourage him to follow the toy.

As with all of our play routines, we want your child to play this game for 10 minutes or longer.

Expand the Game

1. Slowly add a new person to your game. Coach the person ahead of time not to add too many new words or vary the game so much that you lose your child's participation and interest. If your child begins to walk away or have a meltdown, you've probably changed the game too much for her right now. Sometimes a child can handle an adult or a much older child joining in the game, but not a child near her own age. In the beginning adding a sibling, especially one that's very close in age, creates too much jealousy so that your child can't continue to play. In that case, save this game for 1:1 time with you or playtime with another adult.

2. Try a new object.

CAUTION: Please use common sense and parental discretion with this activity. Do not leave the string tied around the toy when you're finished with this game since your child could become tangled or choke.

BLOCKS

Materials:
Any blocks can be used, but my favorites are the larger cardboard blocks that can be stacked into tall towers. Some creative parents keep shoe boxes or other small boxes for stacking.

Great for a Child Who:
Isn't that interested in regular toys yet
Likes to crash into things

How to Play:
Stack a few blocks on top of each other saying, "Block! Block!" Remember to be simple and repetitive with your words. Say, "Block" each time you place a block on top.

When your child is watching, make a big gesture, and knock the blocks over. You can count before you do this to build anticipation or say, "Ready, Set, Go."

Most of the time a child is so surprised that an adult is doing this, he'll want to play.

After the blocks have fallen down, say something like, "Oh no!!!" or "Uh-oh!!"

Have a good laugh, and then begin the routine again.

Many children will try to knock the blocks down after only one or two blocks, and that's okay initially. Don't ruin the fun by scolding your child. Counting to 3 or saying, "Ready-Set- Go!" helps slow them down, but sometimes you just have to build your tower as quickly as you can before a child knocks them down!

Try to get your child to help you build the tower too. Give him a block and point to where he should put it saying, "Block! On top!" If he doesn't place it on top, help him if it doesn't make him too mad.

Child's Goals:
Of course our #1 goal is for your child to participate by knocking over the blocks and laughing hysterically when they fall.

If he's not smiling, laughing, and having a great time, then chances are you're not being fun enough. As I tell every parent and therapist I work with, "Ratchet it up a notch!" He's got to believe you're having FUN playing *with* him.

Secondary goals would be for him to imitate the simple, repetitive sounds and key words you've been saying. Be sure you're not using too many different words during this play routine.

If he's not joining in, but even beginning to watch the blocks fall down, keep trying! Take his hand or his foot and knock the tower over. If you are fun enough, simple enough, and repetitive enough, he will join you in play.

As with all of our play routines, we want your child to play this game for 10 minutes or longer.

Expand the Game

1. Slowly add a new person to your game. Coach the person ahead of time not to add too many new words or vary the game so much that you lose your child's participation and interest. If your child begins to walk away or have a melt down, you've probably changed the game too much for him right now. Sometimes a child can handle an adult or a much older child joining in the game, but not a child near his own age. In the beginning adding a sibling, especially one that's very close in age, creates too much jealousy and stress so that your child can't continue to play. In that case, save this game for 1:1 time or playtime with another adult.

2. Try this game with different blocks or new items like pillows, or even toys that aren't normally stacked such as small cars. This is a great way to expand play with kids who like to line everything up and who get mad when you touch their things.

3. As you're stacking blocks and your child is helping, make this kind of play even more social by asking for a turn. When your child has had several turns with the block, hold your hand out and say, "Give me block," or "My turn?" If he's not giving you the block after several attempts, keep your hand open, and then use your other hand to "help" him place the block in your hand. If this makes him too mad, skip this "sharing" step for now. The most important thing is that he wants to continue to play *with* you.

HATS

Materials:

You can use any kind of hat, and the more hats you have to play with, the better! I especially like to play with hats that are really big or really small for the contrast. If you have one, play this game in front of a large mirror.

Great for a Child Who:

Isn't that interested in regular toys yet

How to Play:

Sit on the floor and say, "Ooooh! Hats!" Place a hat on your head and exaggerate moving around showing it off saying, "Hat. Look! Ooh! Hat!" Pat your head each time you say, "Hat" since this is sign language for hat. If your child doesn't get too upset, help him sign "hat" too.

Other things to do would be to place one that's too small on your head and try to make it fit with great effort saying, "Uh, uh, uh!"

Another fun idea if your child isn't attending that well is to place a hat that's too small on your head, and then pretend to sneeze, so the hat falls off to the floor. Over-exaggerate a huge, "Ah, ah, ah, ah chooooooooo!" I use hats from my Potato Head set for this game.

Lift the hat up and down on your head saying, "Up" and "Down." Try to say these with contrast like high/low voices or loud/soft contrasts to see if you can get a giggle. Some kids seem to respond more when I say, "On" and "Off," so try both sets of words to see which one your child likes more or might try to imitate.

If your child doesn't want to put the hat on himself, see if he'll let you put it on and off his head. Use the same words he liked when you did this on yourself.

Try something unexpected with the hat. Hold it in front of your face then his face to hide to play peek-a-boo. Hide the hat in his shirt and ask, "Where's hat?" Or make a big deal about sitting on it, and ask, "Where's hat?" Place both hands out to the side in a big gesture each time you ask, "Where's hat?"

Child's Goals:

Of course our #1 goal is for your child to participate by putting on and taking off the hats. If she's not smiling and having a good time, then chances are you're not being fun enough. As I tell every parent and therapist I work with, "Ratchet it up a notch!" She's got to know you're having FUN playing *with* her.

Secondary goals would be for him to imitate the simple, repetitive sounds and key words you've been saying. Be sure you're not using too many different words during this play routine.

If she's not joining in, but even beginning to watch you play with the hats, keep trying new things with the hats, or try something different like shoes or sunglasses. If you are fun enough, simple enough, and repetitive enough, she will join you in play.

As with all of our play routines, we want your child to play this game for 10 minutes or longer.

Expand the Game

1. Expand the game to include hats, shoes, and sunglasses.

2. Expand the game to include dolls or a stuffed animal so that you're placing the hat on and off the doll. Hide the doll's face with the hat for a game of peek-a-boo. Make the doll sneeze the hat off, or do other silly things like jump on the hat, try to eat the hat, or wrestle the hat. Beginning with a hat that he's played with is a great way to expand a child's interest to play with a doll or stuffed animal. Once you've played with the hat, move on to feeding the doll with a bottle or cup or a small bowl and spoon.

3. Slowly add a new person to your game. Coach the person ahead of time not to add too many new words or vary the game so much that you lose your child's participation and interest. If your child begins to walk away or have a melt down, you've probably changed the game too much for him right now. Sometimes a child can handle an adult or a much older child joining in the game, but not a child near his own age. In the beginning adding a sibling, especially one that's very close in age, creates so much jealousy and stress that your child can't continue to play. In that case, save this game for 1:1 playtime with you or playtime with another adult.

4. Make this kind of play even more social for asking for a turn. When your child has had several turns with the hat or a shoe, hold your hand out and say, "Give me the hat," or "My turn?" If he's not giving you the hat after several attempts, keep your hand open, and then use your other hand to "help" him place the hat in your hand. If sharing continues to make him too mad, skip this step for now. The most important thing is that he wants to play *with* you.

PHONE

Materials:
You can use any kind of toy phone, but a real cell or cordless phone works best!

Great for a Child Who:
Isn't that interested in regular toys yet
Uses jargon, but not that many real words to talk

How to Play:
Grab the phone excitedly and say, "Hello? Hello?" If a child is not trying to get the phone from me, I hold it out and offer it to him. If he doesn't take it, place the phone in his hand and help him hold it up to his ear. Say, "Hello! Oh, hi!" Exaggerate your words by extending your vowels with "Hiiiiiiiii!" You can pretend that Mommy or Daddy is calling by saying, "Hi Mama," or "Hi Dada." You may also use some filler words here such as, "Uh-oh. Oh yes! No. Okay." Then say, "Bye-bye," and with a big gesture, put the phone down. Use lots of facial expressions and gestures like shaking your head yes or no as you say the corresponding word.

Keep your routine simple and try to stick to the same 3 or 4 words every time you play this game. Many times your child will want to grab the phone and walk around, which is fine, since this is the way a toddler sees adults talk on the phone! Follow him around and then get in front of him to say something like, "Okay! See ya! Bye-bye!" and hang up the phone.

Some parents are hesitant to allow their children to "play" with the phone, but in my experience, in most homes this happens anyway, so embrace this activity as a way to entice your child to interact with you. Many children are interested in my cell phone during therapy sessions, and I work this into our play routines. If the phone happens to ring and I'm not answering the call, it's fun to launch the play routine from a real ring.

Child's Goals:
Of course our #1 goal is for your child to participate by holding the phone up to his ear and looking at you as you supply the words for the call. This is another time when you need to exaggerate and make your facial expressions fun, especially the first few times

when you play so that your child understands this is a game. If your child is not attending, get closer to his face, or hold him on your lap while playing with the phone.

A secondary goal would be for her to imitate the simple, repetitive sounds and key words you've been saying. Many children will begin to say, "Hello" and "Bye" using this game. Be sure you're not using too many different words during this play routine so she can pick out which key words to imitate.

If he's not joining in, but even beginning to act interested in the phone, keep trying. Exaggerate your words and use more actions. Use a big fake laugh like someone has just told you a hilarious story. If you are fun enough, simple enough, and repetitive enough, he will want to join you in play.

As with all of our play routines, we want your child to play this game for 10 minutes or longer.

Expand the Game

1. Add a new person to your game. This is especially true if you've tried this often and are getting no response with this game. Have the other person take the phone from you and "talk." Coach the person ahead of time not to say too many words during the game. Sometimes a slight variation will help your child want to "talk on the phone" too.

2. Make this kind of play even more social by asking for a turn. When your child has had several turns with the phone, hold your hand out and say, "Give me the phone," or "My turn?" If he's not giving you the phone after several attempts, keep your hand open, and then use your other hand to "help" him place the phone in your hand or hold it up to your ear. If sharing continues to make him too mad, skip this step for now. The most important thing is that he wants to play *with* you.

LAUNDRY BASKET

Materials:
Plastic laundry basket

Great for a Child Who:
Isn't that interested in regular toys yet
Likes to fit in small spaces

How to Play:
You'll have to play for a while to determine which routine your child likes best. If you get a negative or no reaction, move on to find a routine he likes.

If he's climbed in, move the basket back and forth and sing one of your beginner songs he likes such as "Rocking, Rocking" or "Row Your Boat."

If your child likes to lie on the floor or hide in small spaces, this is an ideal game. Place the basket over him, knock on the outside saying, "Knock, Knock, Knock! Who's there?" Take it off and say, "Boo" or "It's _____!"

If you have lots of energy or need your work out, help her climb in the basket and pull her through your home giving her a ride. Say, "Ready - Set - Go" to get started, then after pulling her a few feet, abruptly stop and yell, "Stop!" Begin the routine again.

Some children like climbing in and then being dumped out. Move the basket from side to side for each number saying, "1, 2, 3 – GO!" and then dump your child on the floor. Say, "Uh oh" or "Boom" when your child hits the floor. After a big laugh, help him climb back in to begin again.

Child's Goals:
Of course our #1 goal is for your child to participate by smiling, laughing, and wanting to play over and over. If she's not smiling and having a good time, then chances are you're not being fun enough. As I tell every parent and therapist I work with, "Ratchet it up a notch!" She's got to believe you're having FUN playing *with* her.

A secondary goal would be for her to imitate the simple, repetitive sounds and key words you've been using. Be sure you're not saying too many different words during this play routine.

If he's not joining in, but even beginning to act interested, keep trying. Use a different routine. Think about other kinds of games he likes and try to adapt those fun parts to a new game for the laundry basket. If you are fun enough, simple enough, and repetitive enough, he will want to join you.

As with all of our play routines, we want your child to play this game for 10 minutes or longer.

Expand the Game

1. Add a new person to your game. This is especially true if you've tried this often and are getting no response with this game. Coach the person ahead of time not to say too many words during the game. Sometimes a slight variation they use will help your child want to stay and play. Dads are great at coming up with fun ways to use this kind of "toy" in play!

2. Sometimes it's fun when two children are in the basket, but sometimes it turns into a battle! Watch your child's responses and adjust the game accordingly.

3. Vary your play and try one of the other routines to expand the things you can do with your child with the laundry basket. If your child has been hiding under the basket, YOU try to hide under there. Of course you won't fit, but that's the funny part! Laugh and say, "Oh no! Mama's too big!!"

4. Toddlers who like placing things in and then dumping things out of a container will love using the laundry basket for this game. Hold all of the items you're using so that he has to come to you to get more items. This is a very simple way to expand the way a child uses a preferred toy that he won't let anyone else touch.

BLANKET

<u>Materials</u>:
Any blanket or a large piece of Lycra

<u>Great for a Child Who:</u>
Loves his blanket and doesn't want to do anything else

<u>How to Play</u>:
You'll have to play for a while to determine which routine your child likes best. If you get a negative or no reaction, move on to find a routine he likes.

The obvious routine is to hide for "Peek-a- boo" or "Where oh Where?" You might also try "The Night-Night Game" from the Easiest Beginner Routines. Here are some other fun ideas to try:

When a child is holding a blanket and won't let go, initiate a game of Tug of War. Grab the other end with a big grin on your face and twinkle in your eyes. Start with a whisper getting louder on each word, "1….2…..3….PULL!!!!!" Sometimes the child won't know you're pulling and will just let go. If he seems like he wants to continue, playfully toss the blanket back to him, wait until he grabs it, and then begin again. Be careful if your child is standing up since he'll likely fall when you let go or stop pulling, but even this can be fun for kids who like to crash.

If the blanket is large enough, place the blanket under her, and pull her through your home giving her a ride. Say, "1, 2, 3 - Go" to get started, then after pulling her a few feet, abruptly stop and yell, "Stop!" Begin the routine again.

If the blanket is large enough and you have another adult, have your child lie down and swing him in it. Say, "Ready-Set-Go" to get started and swing him back and forth several times. I say, "Swing!" or "Whee!" while swinging a child. If your child likes to count, then count to ten, and stop with a "crash" to the floor. If you're using sign language, this is a great way to get him to use his signs for more, please, go, or swing. For kids who love to crash into things, "throw" them on a couch or bed at the end.

Child's Goals:

Of course our #1 goal is for your child to participate by smiling, laughing, and wanting to play over and over. If she's not smiling and having a good time, then chances are you're not being fun enough. As I tell every parent and therapist I work with, "Ratchet it up a notch!" She's got to know you're having FUN playing *with* her.

This game is a great way to establish eye contact with a child. Often a child will look at me during this game more consistently than any other time. Be sure you're smiling and look like you're having fun too!

A secondary goal would be for your child to imitate the simple, repetitive sounds and key words you've been saying. Be sure you're not using too many different words during this play routine so he can pick out what words to imitate.

If he's not joining in, but even beginning to act interested, keep trying. Use a different routine. Think about other kinds of games he likes and try to adapt those fun parts to a new game. If you are fun enough, simple enough, and repetitive enough, he will want to join you.

As with all of our play routines, we want your child to play this game for 10 minutes or longer.

Expand the Game

1. Add a new person to your game. This is especially true if you've tried this game several times and are getting no response. Coach the person ahead of time not to say too many words during the game. Sometimes a slight variation will help your child want to stay and play. Dads are great at coming up with fun ways to use this kind of "toy" in play!

2. Vary your play and try one of the other routines to expand the things you can do with your child with a blanket. Try new things. Roll him in the blanket, hide other toys he likes under the blanket, make a tent, or play with the blanket like we do with those parachute games. You hold one end while he holds the other, and both of you should "shake" the blanket. Lift the blanket up high over your heads, and then lower the blanket to the floor. This is a fun game for most toddlers, and one that you can use to involve other people too.

DISHES

Materials:
At a minimum you'll need a plastic cup, bowl, and spoon, but using several different cups, bottles, bowls, plates, pans, and utensils of different sizes makes this play more fun. Add one or two items at a time to find just the right number of toys to play with so he's not overwhelmed with too many choices.

Great for a Child Who:
Is not "pretending" to do anything yet
May also help a child learn to use utensils for self-feeding

How to Play:
Playing with dishes in the kitchen while mom cooks is a universal activity, but some children don't know how to do this without a model from an adult. Spread the items out on the floor. Begin by picking up the spoon and stirring in the bowl or pan. Stir loudly so your child will attend to your actions. Say, "STIR!" or "Cook!" while you're doing this. Pretend to take a bite with exaggerated intent and say, "Eat!" or "Bite!" Then say, "Mmmmmm!" or "Yum, yum, yum!." Ask, "More?" and then begin again, repeating your same sequence. Next hold the spoon out to your child and "pretend" to feed him. Say, "Eat" and "Mmm, mmm, mmm" as you offer him the pretend food from your spoon.

Pretend to drink from the cup or bottle with a big, slurpy sound or "Gulp, gulp, gulp," then "Ahhhhhh." Hold the cup out to your child asking, "Want drink?" Hold the cup to his mouth to "help" him drink. When he's finished drinking from the cup, say, "Mommy wants a drink," and then with his hands still on the cup, you should help him move the cup to your mouth so that you can pretend to drink. Continue using all of the items "pretending" to eat, drink, stir, and pour.

Children will typically begin this play by trying to drink from the cup or will put the spoon in their mouths as if they expect something to be there. Some children will become confused and seem to wonder, "Where's the food?" but keep trying to introduce this as a "pretend" game without resorting to adding real food. This kind of play is often the earliest "pretending" we see in toddlers, and these items work well to introduce this concept. Pretending to stir with a spoon and give a parent a drink from a cup is often noted at 12-15 months in children with typically developing language, so it's often an "easier" way to establish "pretending" using these real-life props than with other kinds of toys.

Child's Goals:

Of course our #1 goal is for your child to participate by "pretending" to eat, drink, and stir with the spoon. We also want your child to stay with this kind of play and not move on to other things. Be sure to make it silly and fun with lots of loud "noises" as you're pretending so at the very least your child is noticing you.

Next we want to make this play more "social" by having your child pretend to feed you or give you a drink with the cup without you helping him hold the utensil to your mouth. Make this activity fun for your child by laughing and being very silly and playful.

If she's not smiling and having a good time, then chances are, you are not being fun enough. As I tell every parent and therapist I work with, "Ratchet it up a notch!" She's got to believe you're having FUN playing *with* her.

A secondary goal would be for your child to imitate the simple, repetitive sounds and key words you've been using. Be sure you're not saying too many different words during this play routine so that she knows which words to imitate.

If he's not joining in, but even beginning to act interested, keep trying. Use a different routine. If you are fun enough, simple enough, and repetitive enough, he will want to join you in play.

As with all of our play routines, we want your child to play this game for 10 minutes or longer.

Expand the Game

1. Add a new person to your game. This is especially true if you've tried this game several times and are getting no response. Coach the person ahead of time not to say too many words during the game. Sometimes a slight variation they use will help your child want to stay and play.

2. Add a doll or stuffed animal to your play. Pretend to feed the doll and animal. Use your same sound effects when the doll or animal eat to keep this "social" and keep your child engaged with you.

3. If all else fails, turn the bowl over and hit it with the spoon. Almost any kid likes to "bang." Say, "Bang, bang, bang" as you hit the bowl (or a pan) with the spoon. If hitting the bowl with the spoon seems to be too hard for your child, pat the bottom of the bowl or pan with your hand and say, "Boom! Boom!"

PAPER AIRPLANES

Materials:
Any piece of paper

Great for a Child Who:
Likes to watch fans or bubbles

How to Play:
Fold a piece of paper into a paper airplane. Hold the airplane near your face to help establish eye contact. Throw the paper airplane into the air and say, "Airplane! Whee," or "Fly" exaggerating the vowel sound so that it sounds like, "Wheeeeeeeeeeeeeeee!"

If your child doesn't notice the plane and try to "catch" it, then you should jump up and run over to get it saying, "Where's airplane?" Say, "Look! Airplane! Wheeeee!" Continue to play for several more turns. This game will be a challenge for children with poor visual tracking and attending skills.

If your child gets the airplane, hold out your hand so he can give it to you to fly. Children usually have a hard time getting paper airplanes to fly as well as an adult can, so it makes a great "social" activity since your child needs help. Say, "Give me plane," or "My turn" as you hold out your hand. If he doesn't give you the plane, keep one hand out and open, and use your other hand to "help" him put the plane in your open hand. If giving you the plane makes him too mad and he can't make it fly himself, try to get the plane before your child can, and quickly begin the next turn. You might also try to make two planes so he has one to hold during play. However, when you give a child a duplicate item, he often focuses on the toy and leaves you out of play, and this is not your goal!

If your child has squished the plane or tries to tear up the paper, say, "Oh no!" exaggerating your facial expressions. You might even pretend to cry to get his attention. Beware! Fake crying becomes addictive to some kids and they want to hear you do it over and over. Use this to your advantage!

Begin again with a new piece of paper.

Child's Goals:

Of course our #1 goal is for your child to participate by watching the plane and trying to make it fly.

We also want your child to stay with this kind of play and not move on to other things. Be sure to make it silly and fun with lots of loud "noises" as you're pretending so at the very least your child is noticing you. Use an airplane noise or hold your arms out like a plane's wings and pretend to "fly" yourself.

If she's not smiling and having a good time, then chances are you're not being fun enough. As I tell every parent and therapist I work with, "Ratchet it up a notch!" She's got to know you're having FUN playing *with* her.

A secondary goal would be for your child to imitate the simple, repetitive sounds and key words you've been using. Be sure you're not saying too many different words during this play routine.

If he's not joining in, but even beginning to act interested, keep trying. Use a different routine. If you are fun enough, simple enough, and repetitive enough, he will want to join you in play.

As with all of our play routines, we want your child to play this game for 10 minutes or longer.

Expand the Game

1. Add a new person to your game. This is especially true if you've tried this game several times and are getting no response. Coach the person ahead of time not to say too many words during the game. Sometimes a slight variation they use will help your child want to stay and play.

2. Sometimes a child will like this game, but is so rough on the paper that you only get one flight per airplane. If your child likes this activity, look for a real toy that flies. You might also try to find a toy that shoots balls or discs that your child can't destroy!

SPINNING CHAIR

(Adapted from <u>Giggle Time</u>,
by Susan Aud Sonders)

Materials:

You'll need an office chair that spins, a toddler swing, or you might try it on a Sit and Spin.

Great for a Child Who:

Likes to spin or run

How to Play:

When your child is seated in the chair, stand in front of the chair, place your hands on the arms of the chair and begin to walk around him slowly spinning the chair saying,

Round, and round, and round we go.....

Where we stop

    (Suddenly stop the chair.)

Nobody knows!!!

    (Then move back a little to give the chair a big spin.)

Say, "Whee" or "Spin" as your child is spinning.

Begin again once the chair has stopped.

Child's Goals:

You initially want your child to stay in the chair for the entire game.

Next we want him to connect with you by looking at you, smiling, and laughing during the game. I wait for eye contact at the beginning of the game before I start to spin the chair.

Look for him to initiate or continue this game by bouncing or trying to spin the chair himself.

He may start to look for you to play with him when he climbs up into the chair at other times. If you notice this, drop everything and run over to play your game! He's initiating!

If she's not smiling and having a good time, then chances are, you are not being fun enough. As I tell every parent and therapist I work with, "Ratchet it up a notch!" She's got to know you're having FUN playing *with* her.

A secondary goal would be for your child to imitate the simple, repetitive sounds and key words you've been saying. Be sure you're not using too many different words during this play routine.

If he's not joining in, but even beginning to act interested, keep trying. Use a different routine. Try to sit down and act surprised that he's there. Pick him up and have him sit on your lap while facing you while the both of you spin around in the chair. Dump him out, or you pretend to fall out saying, "Whoa! Uh-oh!" If you are fun enough, simple enough, and repetitive enough, he will want to join you.

As with all of our play routines, eventually you want your child to be able to play this kind of game for 10 minutes or longer.

Expand the Game:

1. Play the game with a new person. This is a new game, so you'll want to have the other person watch you so they play it the same way that you do.

2. In Giggle Time, Susan Aud Sonders plays a version of this game where she rolls the chair away on "Nobody knows." If you have enough room to do this, you may expand the game this way. She also wrestles the child out of the chair at the end which is great for a child who loves to roughhouse.

More Toys...

I can't possibly list every toy I use in therapy sessions, and frankly, that list changes every week since I am constantly adding to my collection. You can find a list of many other toys I like on my website at teachmetotalk.com in the Recommended Toys section. You can see how I play with these in sessions with children on any of my DVDs. I'm also in the process of writing other manuals like this one to address receptive and expressive language delays and speech intelligibility, so please check for more ideas for toys in those publications. In the meantime, here's a short list of my all-time favorites for children who are ready to move to more traditional play with toys:

Bowling Sets   Inflatable Bouncers

Hot Wheels Motorcycle Set   Elefun

Fisher Price Spiral Race Track   Lightning McQueen Race Track

Take Along Thomas   Rev and Go Thomas

Peeks the Clown – Discovery Toys   Ball and Hammer Toys

Tomy Gumball Toy   Tupperware Blocks that open and close

Parents Shape Sorter (at Target)   Potato Heads

Little Linguist by Neurosmith   Inset Wooden Puzzles

Dolls & Accessories   Plastic Foods, Dishes, and Microwave

Pretend Playground, Farm, House with People and Animals

Zoo Animals and Dinosaurs   Puff-a-lump Cookie Monster

Loving Family Play Set   Lucky Ducks

Fishin' Around   Play-doh and accessories

My Little Pony Ferris Wheel with other small animals or characters to place in the seats

FINGERPLAYS AND SONGS

By now your child should be enjoying several easiest beginner routines and early toys with you. Even if it's not quite working like you'd hoped, if you're trying your best, you will begin to see some hint of progress if you don't give up!

Sometimes music reaches a child when words can't. Some children respond to songs long before words begin to make sense to them. If I'm getting nowhere with a child, I always try to sing to capture his or her attention, and it usually works.

Some other children may cover their ears when you sing. Let me reassure you that it's usually <u>not</u> because of your voice! Your child likely has auditory sensitivities and may also react negatively to other noises. Even if this is the case, don't stop singing. Try a different tone singing a little higher or lower, sing softly, and always use fewer words.

I hope that both of you will enjoy these songs and fingerplays. Each page includes:

- The name of the fingerplay or song
- Materials required (if any). Sometimes props help a child understand the words!
- Detailed instructions in "How to Play" including the words and hand motions for each song or fingerplay
- List of child's goals so that you'll know what responses to shoot for, how to help your child advance to a higher level response, and how to measure progress
- Ideas for expanding the activity
- The chapter is organized by difficulty with the easier ones first and by themes.

If your child doesn't seem to enjoy a particular song or fingerplay on your first few attempts, don't give up! I sometimes sing a song many times before a child gives me any indication he likes it. Keep at it. Repetition builds familiarity, and once a child knows the song or fingerplay, he's more likely to want to try to sing or do the hand motions.

If you're not sure about the tunes for some of these songs, many of them are posted on my Youtube channel at youtube.com/user/teachmetotalk, or Google it to hear and see an example.

One last word of advice, get ready to sing and play! Turn off your phone and the TV. Ignore any other distractions. Plaster a big, warm smile on your face and get ready to woo your child into interacting with you. Even if you can't carry a tune in a bucket, I hope you'll try to sing. Remember, sometimes music reaches a child when words can't.

PATTY CAKE

<u>Materials</u>: None

<u>How to Play</u>:
Sit in a chair or on the floor and hold your baby on your lap facing you so your child can see you and you can help him clap.

This classic game has so many different versions. I like this one:

Patty cake, patty cake, baker's man.
>   (Clap hands to rhythm of words.)

Bake me a cake as fast as you can.
>   (Clap hands.)

Pat it out.
>   (Clap faster.)

Roll it up.
>   (Roll hands in a circle.)

And throw it in the pan!
>   (Throw hands up in the air.)

Clap and cheer saying, "Yay!" at the end of the rhyme.

Be sure you're saying the words slowly so your child can learn the words too.

Help your child do the motions until you've played this game for several days or weeks, but stop helping when she begins to try to clap on her own.

Repeat this game several times before moving on to a different activity. Remember, toddlers need lots of repetition to begin to recognize and then learn a new game.

<u>Child's Goals</u>:
Watch his responses. We want him to connect with you by looking at you, smiling, and laughing when you are helping him do the motions. If he doesn't smile, be more fun! Increase your own level of animation. Try a big hug or tickle to get him going.

A main goal for this game is to get him to stay through the entire song. If he tries to wiggle off your lap, try bouncing him on your legs while you say the rhyme. Try making the motions bigger and more fun so he wants to stay. If he likes big endings, try a big flip or tickle or wrestle him to the ground at the end when you are saying, "Yay!"

We want her to do the motions on her own, so stop helping her when she starts to do them herself.

Pretty soon you may start to hear him try to say, "Yay!" or other words from the rhyme on his own. Listen carefully for any word attempt.

As with all of our play routines, eventually you want your child to sing songs with you for 10 minutes or longer.

Expand the Game:

1. Play with a new person. Have the person watch you several times to learn how to play the game exactly like you do.

2. When you see her clapping at other times, initiate the game by asking, "Patty cake?" This will help her learn to initiate the game on her own.

Other Versions:

Patty cake, patty cake, baker's man.
>   (Clap hands to rhythm of words.)

Bake me a cake as fast as you can.
>   (Clap hands.)

Pat it.
>   (Clap faster.)

Prick it.
>   (Tap one index finger to palm of other hand.)

Mark it with a "B."
>   (Draw a B in your palm.)

Put it in the oven for baby and me!
>   (Rub hands together, and then pat your chest on "me.")

SO BIG

<u>Materials</u>: None

<u>How to Play</u>:

Ask your child, "**How big is (child's name)?**"

Lift your own arms up above your head and say, **"Soooooo big!"**

Repeat this game several times in a row.

Most kids need an extra "Wow!" to make this game worthwhile to play. You might try a "reward" at the end like picking your child up and swinging him around when his arms are raised. This may facilitate him using this communicative gesture for other times when he wants to be picked up and held.

If your child doesn't try to hold his arms up when you say, "So Big," gently lift his arms.

Immediately clap and cheer for him saying, "Yay!"

Use Dad or siblings as a model for this too. Get everyone to hold their arms up and say, "Soooooo big!" Encourage everyone to cheer at the end.

Repeat this game 5 or 6 times before moving on to a different activity. Remember, toddlers need lots of repetition to begin to recognize and then learn a new game.

Child's Goals:

At first we want your child to watch you and smile.

Next we want your child to hold up his own arms while he watches you hold your arms up too.

Then we want your child to hold her arms up by herself when she hears, "How big is ___?" without having to see you lift up your arms.

When a child has truly learned this game, he holds his arms up, grins, and looks at his parents to say the words for him.

Other things to try as a "reward" might be to tickle under his arms when he holds them up.

Or you might try your lifting arms up and waving them on "Soooo" and then coming down fast and slapping your legs for "Big." This is effective for kids who like to run and crash into furniture or the wall since it gives them a little of the deep pressure they crave.

Pause before saying, "Big" so that your child might attempt this word.

As with all of our play routines, eventually you want your child to play games and sing songs with you for 10 minutes or longer.

Expand the Game:

1. Have a different person ask, "How big is _____?"

2. Play in a new place. You can ask your child this while he's seated in his car seat, in the grocery store cart, or in his stroller.

ITSY BITSY SPIDER

<u>Materials</u>: None

<u>How to Play</u>:

This is an easy song most parents already know and that babies and toddlers love. When you have your child's attention, begin to sing slowly, and do the following hand motions:

Itsy bitsy spider went up the water spout.

>(Touch your top index finger to your other thumb and remain touching as your bottom index finger and thumb rotate upward to touch again.)

Down came the rain,

>(Wiggle your fingers and move both hands down like it's raining.)

And washed the spider out.

>(Cross both hands in front of you, and then out to the side a couple of times.)

Out came the sun, and dried up all the rain,

>(Make a circle with both arms above your head, and sway to the left side, and then to the right.)

And the itsy bitsy spider went up the spout again.

>(Touch your top index finger to your thumb and remain touching as your bottom index finger and thumb rotate upward to touch again.)

At the end clap and say, "Yay!"

Sing slowly so your child can learn the words and try to sing along with you.

Repeat this song several times before moving on to a different activity. Remember, toddlers need lots of repetition to begin to recognize and then learn a new song.

Child's Goals:

The first goal is for your child to attend to what you're doing, stay with you, and watch your hand movements.

A nice goal would be for your child to begin to hum, bounce along to the rhythm, or even try to sing along.

We do want her to try to imitate these hand motions, but some of them are hard! Many children will come up with their own versions of the hand motions for this song, and that's okay. Help your child perform the hand motions if it doesn't ruin the song for you both.

As with all of our play routines, eventually you want your child to sing songs with you for 10 minutes or longer.

Expand the Game:

1. Sing this song with a new person. Most adults and older children know this song, so it's easy to have another person sing this one and help your child learn how to connect with and play with someone else.

2. Try this song in new places such as at the doctor's office when you're waiting, in the line at the store, or even in the car at a stop light.

3. Singing is a great distraction when you need to head off a meltdown or to redirect your child's attention when he's about to do something he shouldn't.

4. Sing this song when you've seen a real spider (YIKES!) or you've seen a picture of a spider in a book.

TWINKLE, TWINKLE LITTLE STAR

<u>Materials</u>: None

<u>How to Play</u>:
This is another easy song most parents already know. When your child is near you, begin to sing slowly and do the hand motions:

Twinkle, twinkle, little star,
>   (Hold both hands in front of you, and open and close your hands.)

How I wonder what you are.
>   (Point to your temple or forehead.)

Up above the world so high,
>   (Point up to the sky.)

Like a diamond in the sky.
>   (Make a diamond shape with your hands by touching your index fingers and your thumbs.)

Twinkle, twinkle, little star,
>   (Open and close your hands.)

How I wonder what you are!
>   (Point to your temple.)

At the end clap and say, "Yay!"

Sing slowly so your child can learn the words and try to sing along with you.

Repeat this song several times before moving on to a different activity. Remember, toddlers need lots of repetition to begin to recognize and then learn a new song.

I especially like to sing this song at night when a child can see the stars or when we've seen a picture of a star in a book.

Child's Goals:

The first goal is for your child to attend to what you're doing, stay with you for the entire song, and watch your hand movements.

Next we want him to try to imitate these simple hand motions. I help a child perform the motions if it doesn't upset him and ruin the song.

A nice goal would be for your child to begin to hum, bounce along to the rhythm, or even try to sing along.

After singing the song regularly for several days or week, pause at the end of the line for "Twinkle, Twinkle Little…" and see if your child will complete, "Star." Once she's trying to say this, pause at the ends of the other lines too to see if she'll fill in other words.

As with all of our play routines, eventually you want your child to sing songs with you for 10 minutes or longer.

Expand the Game:

1. Have a different person sing this song with your child. Most adults and older children know this song too, so it's easy to have another person sing this one and help your child learn to connect and play with someone else.

2. Try this song in new places such as at the doctor's office when you're waiting, in the line at the store, or even in the car at a stop light.

3. Singing is a great distraction when you need to head off a meltdown or to redirect your child's attention when he's about to do something he shouldn't.

WHEELS ON THE BUS

<u>Materials</u>: None

<u>How to Play</u>:
Slowly sing to your child:

The wheels on the bus go round and round,
Round and round, round and round.
The wheels on the bus go round and round,
All through the town.

      (Roll hands over each other on first lines. Each time you sing, "All through the town," cross one arm over to the opposite side of your body, point your finger toward the ground, and move your arm in a big circle over your head to finish by your side.)

The wipers on the bus go, "Swish, swish, swish,
Swish, swish, swish, swish, swish, swish."
The wipers on the bus go, "Swish, swish, swish,"
All through the town.

      (Put arms together in front of you and move your arms back and forth and 'swish' like windshield wipers.)

The door on the bus goes open and shut,
Open and shut, open and shut.
The door on the bus goes open and shut,
All through the town.

      (Hold both hands out to each side of your body for "open," and then close them in a clap for "shut.")

The horn on the bus goes, "Beep, beep, beep,
Beep, beep, beep, beep, beep, beep."
The horn on the bus goes, "Beep, beep, beep,"
All through the town.

      (Pretend to honk the horn by pushing with one hand in front of your body.)

The people on the bus go, "Up and down,
up and down, up and down."
The people on the bus go, "Up and down,"
All through the town.

> (Sit up on your knees and raise both arms for "up," then sit back down on the floor for "down.")

The baby on the bus says, "Wah, wah, wah!
Wah, wah, wah, wah, wah, wah!"
The baby on the bus says, "Wah, wah, wah!"
All through the town.

> (Sign "baby" by rocking your arms as if rocking a baby. On "Wah" rub your eyes with both fisted hands like the baby is crying.)

The Mommy on the bus says, "Shh, shh, shh,
Shh, shh, shh, shh, shh, shh."
The Mommy on the bus says, "Shh, shh, shh,"
All through the town.

> (Put pointer finger to mouth to 'shhh.')

The Daddy on the bus says, "I love you,
I love you, I love you."
The Daddy on the bus says, "I love you,"
All through the town.

> (Point to your chest or eye for "I," cross your arms in front of your body for "love," and point to your baby for "you.")

Child's Goals:

The first goal is for your child to attend to what you're doing, stay with you, and watch your hand movements.

We want your child to begin to copy the hand motions and eventually try to sing the words. If it doesn't ruin the song, help him perform the actions.

This is a long song! You don't have to sing every verse, every time. I always start with the first verse and then do the verses a particular child enjoys most.

TWO LITTLE BLACKBIRDS

<u>Materials</u>: None

<u>How to Play</u>:

When your child is paying attention to you, begin this finger play with both hands behind your back to build excitement, and then quickly bringing out your index fingers to chant,

Two little blackbirds sitting on a hill,

(Hold up two index fingers in front of body.)

One named Jack. One named Jill.

(Move one index finger up/down for Jack, then the other one for Jill.)

Fly Away Jack. Fly away Jill.

(Hide one hand behind back for Jack, then hide the other hand for Jill.)

Come back Jack. Come back Jill.

(Bring first hand back for Jack, then next hand back for Jill.)

Be sure you're saying the words slowly so your child can learn the words too.

After your child has watched you do this fingerplay for a couple of days, help your child begin to do the motions. Stop helping when he begins to point his fingers on his own.

Repeat this game several times before moving on to a different activity. Remember, toddlers need lots of repetition to begin to recognize and then learn a new fingerplay.

I like to play this game when a child sees a bird outside or in a book.

Child's Goals:

The first goal is for your child to attend to you, stay with you, and watch your hand movements.

The primary goal of this fingerplay is for your child to try to perform these simple hand motions. If it doesn't ruin the game, help him hold up his fingers. Stop helping him when he tries to do this on his own.

As with all of our play routines, eventually you want your child to sing songs with you for 10 minutes or longer.

Expand the Game:

1. Try the fingerplay with a new person. If this is a new game, you'll want to have the other person watch you so they play it the same way that you do.

2. Try this fingerplay in a new place, especially when you're outside and have seen a bird.

3. Singing is a great distraction when you need to head off a meltdown or to redirect your child's attention when he's about to do something he shouldn't.

IF YOU'RE HAPPY AND YOU KNOW IT

<u>Materials</u>: None

<u>How to Play</u>:
Sing to your child,

If you're happy and you know it, clap your hands.
> (Clap hands twice.)

If you're happy and you know it, clap your hands.
> (Clap hands twice.)

If you're happy and you know it,
Then your face will surely show it.
> (Point to your smiling mouth with both index fingers.)

If you're happy and you know it, clap your hands.
> (Clap hands twice.)

<u>Other verses:</u>
Stomp your feet
Shout "Hooray"
Tap your toe
Nod/Pat your head
Rub your tummy
Close your eyes
Any other movement your child likes!

Be sure you're singing the words slowly so your child can learn the words too.

This song can be as long or as short as your child can handle. For most children I pick 3 verses they seem to like and then repeat them a couple of times before moving on to a different activity. Remember, toddlers need lots of repetition to begin to recognize and then learn a new song. Add verses only when your child knows and loves the song.

Child's Goals:

The first goal is for your child to attend to what you're doing, stay with you, and watch your hand movements.

The primary goal of this song is for your child to perform the actions. If it doesn't ruin the song, help him imitate you.

As with all of our play routines, eventually you want your child to sing songs with you for 10 minutes or longer.

Expand the Game:

1. Sing this song with a new person. Most people know this song too, but you'll have to tell them which verses your child likes.

2. Try this song in a new place when you're sitting and waiting.

3. Change the "emotion" word or "physical state" word to expand your child's vocabulary. Try:

If you're sad and you know it, cry.
>   (Young children love to imitate crying!)

If you're mad and you know it, stomp your feet.
>   (Make an angry face.)

If you're sleepy and you know it, go to bed.
>   (Close your eyes, place both hands together on one side of your face, and then tilt your head as if sleeping. Snore for your action. This is also funny for kids!)

If you're thirsty and you know it, take a drink.
>   (Sign "Drink" and slurp and then "Ahhh" for action.)

If you're hungry and you know it, eat your food.
>   ("Yum – Yum" while rubbing tummy.)

4. Singing is a great distraction when you need to head off a meltdown or to redirect your child's attention when he's about to do something he shouldn't. The motions for this song are easy too, so it's a great way to redirect a child's energy and focus!

OPEN SHUT THEM

Materials: None

How to Play:
Hold both hands with big, open palms facing outward and sing,

Open, shut them.
> (For "open," hold both hands with big, open palms facing outward. For "shut them," close your hands into fists.)

Open, shut them.
> (Repeat same actions.)

Give a little clap.
> (Clap hands.)

Open, shut them.
> (Same open/shut actions.)

Put them in your lap.
> (Fold hands and put them in your lap.)

Creep them, creep them,
Creep them, creep them,
> (Starting at the tummy, slowly 'creep' fingers up toward the face.)

Right up to your chin,
> (Point to your chin.)

Open up your mouth,
> (Open your mouth.)

But do not let them in.
> (Just as it looks like you're going to put fingers into mouth, quickly run fingers back down body toward tummy.)

Be sure you're singing the words slowly so your child can learn the words too.

After your child has watched you do this fingerplay for a couple of times, help your child begin to do the motions. Stop helping when he begins to open and close his hands on his own.

Repeat this fingerplay several times before moving on to a different activity. Remember, toddlers need lots of repetition to begin to recognize and then learn a new game.

Child's Goals:

The first goal is for your child to attend to what you're doing, stay with you, and watch your hand movements.

The primary goal of this song is for your child to imitate these easy hand motions. If it doesn't ruin the song, help him perform the motions until he can do them on his own.

As with all of our play routines, eventually you want your child to sing songs with you for 10 minutes or longer.

Expand the Game:

1. Sing this song with a new person. If this is a new song, you'll want to have the other person watch you first so they sing it the same way that you do.

2. Try this song in a new place when you're sitting and waiting.

3. Singing is a great distraction when you need to head off a meltdown or to redirect your child's attention when he's about to do something he shouldn't.

HEAD, SHOULDERS, KNEES, AND TOES

<u>Materials</u>: None

<u>How to Play</u>:
You can sing this song while sitting on the floor with your legs stretched out in front of you, but it's more fun if you're standing. Touch each body part with both hands as you sing,

Head, shoulders, knees and toes, knees and toes,
Head, shoulders, knees and toes, knees and toes,
Eyes and ears and mouth and nose,
Head and shoulders, knees and toes, knees and toes.

Be sure you're saying the words slowly so your child can keep up and learn the words too! After your child has watched you sing this song for a couple of times, help your child begin to do the motions. Stop helping when he begins to try to do the motions on his own.

Repeat this song several times before moving on to a different activity. Remember, toddlers need lots of repetition to begin to recognize and then learn a new game.

<u>Child's Goals</u>:
The first goal is for your child to attend to what you're doing, stay with you, and watch your hand movements.

The primary goal of this song is for your child to touch the appropriate body part on her body.

Many children will begin to sing, "Head" and "Toes" since these are the first and last words of the line that's repeated several times.

As with all of our play routines, eventually you want your child to sing songs with you for 10 minutes or longer.

<u>Expand the Game:</u>
Sing with a new person and in new places. This is a great song to help a child become interested in pointing to body parts when you ask. After the song I always teasingly ask, "Where's your head," and then follow up with the other body parts too.

I'M A LITTLE TEAPOT

Materials: None

How to Play:
When you have your child's attention, begin to slowly sing,

I'm a little teapot
Short and stout.
Here is my handle.
> (Put one hand on your hip to form a "handle.")

Here is my spout.
> (Hold other arm out and curve it to make a "spout.")

When I get all steamed up,
Then I shout.
Just tip me over and pour me out!
> (Lean over to the side with your spout as if you're pouring out your tea.)

Child's Goals:
The first goal is for your child to attend to what you're doing, stay with you, and watch your movements.

The primary goal of this song is for your child to perform the motions.

As with all of our play routines, eventually you want your child to sing songs with you for 10 minutes or longer.

Expand the Game:
1. Play the game with a new person. Most adults will remember this song. Have the other person watch you first so they play it the same way that you do.

2. I like to play this game when we're playing with dishes or are in the kitchen and pouring real drinks.

3. Try this game in a new place.

JINGLE BELLS

<u>Materials</u>: None required, but I often use two sets of bells, one for the child and one for me.

<u>How to Play</u>:
This is a Christmas song, but I sing it all year! Shake your bells as you sing,

Jingle bells, jingle bells,
Jingle all the way.
Oh what fun it is to ride
In a one-horse open sleigh! Hey!
Jingle bells, jingle bells,
Jingle all the way.
Oh what fun it is to ride
In a one-horse open sleigh! Hey!

I shout, "Hey!" and throw my hands up in the air to get a bigger reaction each time I shout, "Hey!"

Be sure you're singing the words very slowly so your child can learn the words too.

After your child has watched you sing this song a couple of times, help your child begin to hold up his hands for "Hey!" Stop helping when he can do this on his own.

Repeat this song several times before moving on to a different activity. Remember, toddlers need lots of repetition to begin to recognize and then learn a new song.

<u>Child's Goals</u>:

The first goal is for your child to attend to what you're doing, stay with you, and watch your hand movements.

If you're using bells, we want your child to shake her bells. Help her if it doesn't ruin the song.

The primary goal of this song is for your child to say, "Hey!" After she knows the song, when you get to that word, pause and look at her expectantly as if it's her turn to say, "Hey!"

There's a verse to this song below, but the chorus is the most fun and the part many toddlers will try to sing.

As with all of our play routines, eventually you want your child to be able to sing songs with you for 10 minutes or longer.

Expand the Game:

1. Almost everyone knows this song. Sing this song with new people, and it's a fun one for a group.

2. Try this song in a new place.

3. If you hear bells, sing this song to help your child make the connection.

4. Singing is a great distraction when you need to head off a meltdown or to redirect your child's attention when he's about to do something he shouldn't.

5. Here's the first verse too:

Dashing through the snow,
In a one-horse open sleigh,
O'er the fields we go,
Laughing all the way, ha, ha, ha!
Bells on bobtails ring,
Making spirits bright,
What fun it is to ride and sing,
A sleighing song tonight! Oh!

Many children will try to imitate the laughing phrase, "Ha ha ha." I put my hand up to my mouth as I sing this line, and toddlers will try to imitate that action too.

HAPPY BIRTHDAY

<u>Materials</u>: None required, but I usually sing this in context whenever I'm playing and have a present or pretend cake. I like to make a pretend cake from Play-doh complete with a pretend play-doh candle. You could even use a real candle and light it for more realistic fun.

<u>How to Play</u>:
Slowly and eagerly sing,

Happy Birthday to You
Happy Birthday to You
Happy Birthday Dear (name)
Happy Birthday to You.

Pretend to blow out the candle and then clap and say, "Yay!"

<u>Child's Goals:</u>
The first goal is for your child to attend to what you're doing, stay with you, and watch you.

We also want your child to try to blow out the candle. Using a real candle several times first will help him learn to do this, especially if he doesn't have lots of experience with birthday parties yet.

Another goal for this song is for your child to try to sing along. Many children will try to sing, "You" since it's at the end of the line several times in the song.

As with all of our play routines, eventually you want your child to sing songs with you for 10 minutes or longer.

<u>Expand the Game:</u>
1. Sing this song and play your version of this game with a new person. You'll want to have the other person watch you first so they play it the same way that you do.

2. Sing this song for several weeks before your child's birthday or any other birthday party so that she's ready for the song and knows what to expect.

3. Your child may enjoy this song so much; he'll probably want to keep playing for months after his birthday!

JACK IN THE BOX

<u>Materials:</u> None

<u>How to Play:</u>
This is another toddler favorite! Try this simple game, especially if your child has had difficulty imitating the hand motions in other songs. The actions for this song involve a child's entire body.

Jack in the Box

    (Crouch or squat down on floor.)

Sits so still

Won't you come out?

Yes, I will!!!

    (Jump up and hold both arms up in the air.)

<u>Child's Goals:</u>
The first goal is for your child to attend to what you're doing, stay with you, and watch your movements.

The primary goal of this song is for your child to imitate these simple movements. If it doesn't ruin the game, help him crouch down, and then jump up.

As with all of our play routines, eventually you want your child to sing songs with you for 10 minutes or longer.

<u>Expand the Game:</u>
1. Play the game with a new person. Since this is a new game, you'll want to have the other person watch you so they play it the same way that you do.

2. Help your child learn to initiate by beginning this game when you see him squatting down at other times.

3. Say this rhyme when you're playing with a real Jack in the Box toy to help your child make the connection.

ANIMALS ON THE FARM

Materials:

Small, plastic farm animals to use as props

How to Play:

This song may be easier for a child to try to sing than "Old MacDonald" since the animal sounds are so repetitive. Hold up each animal by your face as you sing about it. This helps a child begin to look at you.

Sing slowly (but energetically!) to the tune of "Wheels on the Bus."

Cows on the farm say, "Moo, moo, moo.

Moo, moo, moo. Moo, moo, moo."

Cows on the farm say, "Moo, moo, moo,"

All day long.

Horses - Neigh

Pigs – Oink

Sheep – Baa

Chicken – Bock

Ducks - Quack

Turkeys - Gobble

Dogs – Woof

Cats – Meow

Be sure you're singing the words slowly so your child can learn the words too and try to join in as you sing.

Sing a few different verses of this game before moving on to a different activity. Remember, toddlers need lots of repetition to begin to recognize and then learn a new song.

I usually sing this song when we're playing with a farm set, a farm puzzle, or see a picture of farm animals. If you're using a book, point to the picture you're singing about before and during that verse. I do prefer to use the plastic animals since I can hold them up by my mouth and face to encourage eye contact.

If I'm losing a child's interest during the song, I make the animal "sing" by his mouth, or give him a kiss, or eat his fingers, or hide his shirt, or stand on his head, etc...

Child's Goals:

The first goal is for your child to attend to what you're doing, stay with you, and watch you hold the animal or point to the picture.

The primary goal of this song is for your child to imitate the animal sound as you sing. Children have to imitate the sound many times before they are able to answer a question such as, "What does the cow say?"

Before you begin a new verse, ask, "Who's next?" and have your child pick up or point to the next animal. Help him grab or point to an animal if he doesn't do it on his own.

As with all of our play routines, eventually you want your child to sing songs with you for 10 minutes or longer.

Expand the Game:

1. Sing with a new person and in new places. If you happen to be at a place with REAL animals, sing this song, since this is a nice way to help your child make the connection.

2. This song might also be a way to help a child stay with you to look at pictures in a book about the farm rather than reading a long story. Excitedly point to a picture of an animal, say the animal's name, and then begin your song.

OLD MACDONALD

Materials:
Small, plastic farm animals to use as props

How to Play:
Hold up each animal by your face as you sing about it.

Old MacDonald had a farm,
E-I-E-I-O!
And on that farm he had some cows,
E-I-E-I-O!
With a moo-moo here,
And a moo-moo there.
Here a moo, there a moo,
Everywhere a moo-moo.
Old MacDonald had a farm,
E-I-E-I-O!

Horse - Neigh

Pig – Oink

Sheep – Baa

Chicken – Bock

Duck - Quack

Turkey - Gobble

Dog – Woof

Cat - Meow

Be sure you're singing the words slowly so your child can learn the words too. Many children will try to sing, "E I E I O."

Sing several verses of this song before moving on to a different activity. Remember, toddlers need lots of repetition to begin to recognize and then learn a new song.

Child's Goals:

The first goal is for your child to attend to what you're doing, stay with you, and watch you sing or use your props or point to the picture of the animal.

The primary goal of this song is for your child to imitate the animal sound as you sing. Children have to imitate the sound before they are able to answer a question such as, "What does the cow say?"

Before you begin a new verse, ask, "Who's next?" and have your child pick up or point to the next animal.

As with all of our play routines, eventually you want your child to be able to sing songs with you for 10 minutes or longer.

Expand the Game:

1. Sing with a new person and in new places. If you happen to be at a place with REAL animals, sing this song, since this is a nice way to help your child make the connection.

2. This song might also be a way to help a child stay with you to look at pictures in a book about the farm rather than reading a long story.

3. If your child likes this song, but can't sing along yet, try the previous song, "Animals on the Farm."

3. You might also try this version with zoo animals,

Old MacDonald had a zoo,
E-I-E-I-U!
And on that zoo he had some lions,
E-I-E-I-U!
With a roar-roar here,
And a roar-roar there
Here a roar, there a roar,
Everywhere a roar-roar.
Old MacDonald had a zoo,
E-I-E-I-U!

Sometimes I am challenged to think what sounds to sing for zoo animals! Try monkeys, elephants, snakes, bears, birds, and any other animal you can come up with for this one!

BABY BUMBLEBEE

<u>Materials</u>: None

<u>How to Play</u>:
This is another toddler favorite.

I'm bringing home my baby bumblebee,
Won't my mommy be so proud of me,
      (Cup hands together as if holding a bee.)
I'm bringing home my baby bumblebee,
Ouch! It stung me!
      (Point to your hand or shake hands as if just stung.)

I'm squishing up my baby bumblebee,
Won't my mommy be so proud of me,
      (Twist and turn palms to "squish" the bee.)
I'm squishing up my baby bumblebee,
Ooh! It's yucky!
      (Open up hands to look at the mess.)

I'm wiping off my baby bumblebee,
Won't my mommy be so proud of me,
      (Wipe hands on shirt.)
I'm wiping off my baby bumblebee,
Now my mommy won't be mad at me!
      (Hold hands up to show they are clean.)

Sing the words slowly so your child can learn the words too.

After your child has watched you do this fingerplay for a couple of days, help your child begin to do the motions. Stop helping when he begins to try to do the motions on his own.

Repeat at least the first verse of this song several times before moving on to a different activity. Remember, toddlers need lots of repetition to begin to recognize and then learn a new game.

Child's Goals:

The first goal is for your child to attend to what you're doing, stay with you, and watch your hand movements.

The primary goal of this song is for your child to imitate these simple hand motions. If it doesn't ruin the song, help him perform these.

Once you've sung the song many times, some children will try to sing, "Bee" if you pause after you sing, "I'm bringing home my baby bumble…."

You could also pause on the next line for your child to fill in and sing, "Me."

As with all of our play routines, eventually you want your child to be able to sing songs with you for 10 minutes or longer.

Expand the Game:

1. Sing this song with a new person. If this is a new song, you'll want to have the other person watch you first so they sing it the same way that you do.

2. I like to sing this song outside when we've seen a bumblebee or when we're looking at pictures in a book and see a bee.

3. Try this song in a new place like waiting in line.

4. Singing is a great distraction when you need to head off a meltdown or to redirect your child's attention when he's about to do something he shouldn't.

FIVE IN THE BED

<u>Materials</u>: None

<u>How to Play</u>:
This is a cute song to sing with your little one, but maybe not at bedtime!

There were five in the bed
> (Hold up 5 fingers.)

And the little one said,
> (Hold out your index finger and thumb close together for "little.")

"Roll over, roll over."
> (Make two fists and roll them over each other in front of your body.)

So they all rolled over
> (Continue rolling.)

And one fell out!
> (Hold up 1 finger and then clap loudly on "Out!")

Continue singing verses substituting 4, 3, and 2.

Last verse:

There was one in the bed
> (Hold up 1 finger.)

And the little one said,
> (Hold out your index finger and thumb close together for "little.")

"All mine!"
> (Stretch both arms out wide to each side.)

"Good night!"
> (Cross both arms over chest.)

Be sure you're singing the words slowly so your child can learn the words too.

After your child has watched you do this fingerplay for a couple of days, help your child begin to do the motions. Stop helping when he begins to try to do the motions on his own.

This is a long song! Some children won't be able to sit through the entire song more than once. If your child likes this one, sing this song a couple of times before moving on to a different activity. Remember, toddlers need lots of repetition to begin to recognize and then learn a new song.

Child's Goals:

The first goal is for your child to attend to what you're doing, stay with you, and watch your hand movements.

The primary goal of this song is for your child to try to perform these hand motions. The easiest ones for him to try would be rolling his hands for, "Roll over" and clapping on,"Out!" If it doesn't ruin the song, help him with the hand motions.

As with all of our play routines, eventually you want your child to sing songs with you for 10 minutes or longer.

Expand the Game:

1. Sing the song with a new person. If this is a new song, you'll want to have the other person watch you first so they play it the same way that you do.

2. Try this song in a new place.

3. Singing is a great distraction when you need to head off a meltdown or to redirect your child's attention when he's about to do something he shouldn't.

4. There are really cute versions of this song performed by a preschool class on YouTube. Watch those for more ideas.

5 LITTLE MONKEYS JUMPING ON THE BED

Materials: None, but if your child has a stuffed or plastic monkey, you could use this as a prop.

How to Play:

This is a favorite song for toddlers and preschoolers. Use the same hand motions for every verse.

Five little monkeys jumping on the bed.
     (Hold up 5 fingers.)
One fell off and bumped his head.
     (Place both hands on your head.)
Mama called the doctor and the doctor said,
     (Place your hand on your ear like you're talking on the phone.)
"No more monkeys jumping on the bed!"
     (Shake your index finger and/or shake your head "No.")

Sing a verse for 4, 3, 2, and then 1 monkey.

Be sure you're saying the words slowly so your child can learn the words too.

This is a long song! Some children won't be able to sit through the entire song more than once. If your child likes this one, sing this song a couple of times before moving on to a different activity. Remember, toddlers need lots of repetition to begin to recognize and then learn a new song.

Child's Goals:

The first goal is for your child to attend to what you're doing, stay with you, and watch your hand movements.

Next we want him to try to imitate the hand motions. If it doesn't ruin the song, help him perform the motions.

As with all of our play routines, eventually you want your child to sing songs with you for 10 minutes or longer.

Expand the Game:

1. Sing this song with a new person and in new places.

2. I like to sing this one while kids are jumping on the bed, floor, or on a trampoline.

3. I like to sing this song when we've seen a toy monkey or a picture of one. If you're at the zoo, by all means, sing this song to help your child make the connection!

4. If your child likes this song, try the next song about monkeys too.

5. Singing is a great distraction when you need to head off a meltdown or to redirect your child's attention when he's about to do something he shouldn't.

5 LITTLE MONKEYS SWINGING IN A TREE

<u>Materials</u>: None

<u>How to Play</u>:
Watch a cute version on my YouTube channel. Use the same hand motions for each verse.

Five little monkeys swinging in a tree
> (Hold up 5 fingers and sway side to side.)

Teasing Mr. Alligator, "Can't catch me....can't catch me."
> (Place each thumb in your ear, spread your fingers wide, and alternate moving your hands up and down like you are "teasing.")

Along came Mr. Alligator, quiet as can be
> (Say this part quietly and slowly to build anticipation. Place both hands together in front of you and move them move them slowly side to side like an alligator is swimming.)

And snapped that monkey right out of that tree!
> (Extend your arms to make an open alligator's mouth with one hand on top and one on bottom, and then CLAP loudly on the word "snapped.")

Sing the remaining verses for 4, 3, 2, and then 1 monkey.

Be sure you're saying the words slowly so your child can learn the words too.

After your child has watched you do this fingerplay for a couple of days, help your child begin to do the motions. Stop helping when he begins to try to do the motions on his own.

This is a long song! Some children won't be able to sit through the entire song more than once. If your child likes this one, sing this song a couple of times before moving on to a different activity. Remember, toddlers need lots of repetition to begin to recognize and then learn a new song.

Child's Goals:

The first goal is for your child to attend to what you're doing, stay with you, and watch your hand movements.

The primary goal of this song is for your child to try to imitate these simple hand motions. If it doesn't ruin the song, help him do the motions.

Your child might also try to "sing" along, even if it's not with words yet.

Pause at the ends of lines to see if your child can fill in a word, especially for "me" and "tree" since these are frequently occurring words in this song.

As with all of our play routines, eventually you want your child to sing songs with you for 10 minutes or longer.

Expand the Game:

1. Sing with a new person and in new places. Older children often know and love this song! If this is a new song, you'll want to have the other person watch you first so they sing it the same way that you do.

2. If your child likes to sing 5 Little Monkeys Jumping on the Bed, alternate these songs.

3. I like to sing this song when we've seen a toy monkey or a picture of one. If you're at the zoo, by all means, sing this song to help your child make the connection!

4. Singing is a great distraction when you need to head off a meltdown or to redirect your child's attention when he's about to do something he shouldn't.

TEN GREEN SPECKLED FROGS

<u>Materials</u>: None required.

I like to use small, plastic frogs to "jump" into a little bowl of water, or copy and laminate pictures of frogs for a visual aid for this traditional preschool song.

<u>How to Play</u>:

You can hear the tune for this song by watching the video on Youtube.

Ten green speckled frogs

Sitting on a speckled log

Eating the most delicious bugs,

Yum, yum!

    (Rub tummy.)

One jumped into the pool

Where it was nice and cool

Now there are nine green speckled frogs.

Sing until all your frogs have jumped away.

Sing the words slowly so your child can learn the words too, but there are lots of words in this song that may not make sense to a child with language delays.

This is a long song! You may only be able to sing it once before you need to move on to a new activity. But remember, toddlers need lots of repetition to begin to recognize and then learn a new song.

Child's Goals:

The first goal is for your child to attend to what you're doing, stay with you, and watch your hand movements.

This song may have too many words for some children, and they may not be able to sit through the entire song. You may need to shorten it for 5 frogs, or even 3 frogs, so that your child stays with you.

I say, "Ribbet, ribbet," after each verse too, which helps some kids stay with me while I sing the entire verse.

As with all of our play routines, eventually you want your child to sing songs with you for 10 minutes or longer.

Expand the Game:

1. Sing this song with a new person. If this is a new song, you'll want to have the other person watch you first so they sing it the same way that you do.

2. Sing this song when you see a real frog or a picture of one.

3. Singing is a great distraction when you need to head off a meltdown or to redirect your child's attention when he's about to do something he shouldn't.

SKINNAMARINK

Materials: None

How to Play:

Each time you sing the first "Skinna..." line, wave your right hand, and then each time you sing the second "Skinna" line, wave your left hand.

Skinnamarinky dinky dink
Skinnamarinky do,
I love you!

> (Point to your chest or your eye for "I," cross your arms across your chest for "love," and point to your child for "you.")

Skinnamarinky dinky dink
Skinnamarinky do,
I love you!

> (Repeat the same motions.)

I love you in the morning,

> (Hold both arms up over your head with your hands clasped like a big sun.)

And in the afternoon,

> (Move your clasped arms down in front of you like the sun is going down.)

I love you in the evening,

> (Continue to move your clasped arms all the way down to the floor.)

Underneath the moon.

> (Now put your arms back over your head like the moon has risen.)

Skinnamarinky dinky dink
Skinnamarinky do,
I love you!

> (Repeat the same motions.)

I LOVE YOU!

> (Grab your child and give her a big kiss!)

This song has some difficult sound combinations, so be sure you're singing the words slowly so your child can learn the words too.

After your child has watched you sing this song for a couple of days, help your child begin to do the motions. Stop helping when he begins to try to do the motions on his own.

Repeat this song several times before moving on to a different activity. Remember, toddlers need lots of repetition to begin to recognize and then learn a new song.

Child's Goals:

The first goal is for your child to attend to what you're doing, stay with you, and watch your hand movements.

The primary goal of this song is for your child to try to imitate these simple hand motions. If it doesn't ruin the song, help him perform the motions.

This song has difficult words to pronounce, but many children will try, long before they can actually say them!

I love this song since it gives your child extra practice saying, "I love you." Your child may hum or try to say this phrase for the first time to you during this song!

As with all of our play routines, eventually you want your child to sing songs with you for 10 minutes or longer.

Expand the Game:

1. Sing this song with a new person and in new places. If this is a new song, you'll want to have the other person watch you first so they sing it the same way that you do.

2. Parents often like this sweet song so much that they sing it every night as a part of their bedtime routine.

3. When I ran a language playgroup program, we used this song every day as our closing circle time activity.

4. Singing is a great distraction when you need to head off a meltdown or to redirect your child's attention when he's about to do something he shouldn't.

BICYCLE SONG   (Adapted from Kate Hensler, DI)

Materials: None, but if your child is playing with or riding a bike, this is a cute song to sing.

How to Play:

Move your hands like you're pedaling a bike. My friend Kate likes to play this game when she and a child are lying on their backs. Put your feet up in the air and pretend to pedal. Sing,

I like to ride my bicycle. I ride it to and fro.
And when I see the big green light, I know it's time to go.
I like to ride my bicycle. I bought it at the shop,
But when I see the big red light, I know it's time to stop!

Child's Goals:

The first goal is for your child to attend to what you're doing, stay with you, and watch you do your hand (or foot!) motions.

The primary goal of this song is for your child to try to participate by "pedaling" his hands or feet.

You could also sign the words "go" and "stop" at the appropriate time in the song.

After you've sung this song for a few days or weeks, pause to see if your child will fill in the words for "go" and "stop."

As with all of our play routines, eventually you want your child to sing songs with you for 10 minutes or longer.

Expand the Game:

1. Sing this song with a new person. Since this is a new song, you'll want to have the other person watch you first so they sing it and play the same way that you do.

2. Try this song in a new place. If you're outside and see someone riding a bike, sing this song to help your child link meaning to the real event.

CLAP AND KICK

Materials: None

How to Play:
I often start this game when a child is lying on his back. It doesn't matter which verse you sing first, so if his feet are closer, start with "Kick." Sing and perform the appropriate motions,

Clap, clap, clap your hands. Clap our hands together.
Clap, clap, clap your hands. Clap our hands together.

Kick, Kick, kick your feet. Kick our feet together.
Kick, Kick, kick your feet. Kick our feet together.

Stomp, stomp, stomp your feet. Stomp our feet together.
Stomp, stomp, stomp your feet. Stomp our feet together.

Child's Goals:
The first goal is for your child to attend to what you're doing and stay with you.

I often sing this song for weeks while I perform the motions on a child using his feet and hands. After I've sung it a few times and think he's recognized the song, I pause and see if he will continue the motion as my cue to keep singing.

You can also perform the hand/foot motions yourself and wait for your child to imitate you.

As with all of our play routines, eventually you want your child to sing songs with you for 10 minutes or longer.

Expand the Game:
1. Play the game with a new person. Since this is a new game, you'll want to have the other person watch you so they play it the same way that you do.

2. Try this game in a new place.

3. This is a fun song for kids who like to spend lots of times on their backs.

CLAP, TWO, THREE, FOUR!

<u>Materials</u>: None

<u>How to Play</u>:
When your child is paying attention to you, or has just finished clapping for something else, introduce this chant,

Clap, two, three, four, five, six, seven.

>   (Clap hands)

Shake, two, three, four, five, six, seven.

>   (Shake hands/fingers)

Slap, two, three, four, five, six, seven.

>   (Slap legs/knees)

Roll, two, three, four, five, six, seven.

>   (Rotate fist over fist in front of body)

Snap, two, three, four, five, six, seven.

>   (Snap fingers)

Tap, two, three, four, five, six, seven.

>   (Pound fists one on top of the other)

Push, two, three, four, five, six, seven.

>   (Push hands forward)

Clap, two, three, four, five, six, seven.

>   (Clap hands)

Be sure you're saying the words slowly so your child can learn the words too.

After your child has watched you do this fingerplay for a couple of days, help your child begin to do the motions. Stop helping when he begins to try to do the motions on his own.

This is a long song, so don't try to do all of the verses at first. Repeat the first couple of verses a few times before moving on to a different activity. Remember, toddlers need lots of repetition to begin to recognize and then learn a new fingerplay.

Child's Goals:

The first goal is for your child to attend to what you're doing, stay with you, and watch your hand movements.

The primary goal for this game is for your child to imitate the different hand motions. Building imitation of motor movements, such as the varied hand motions for this song, is a prerequisite for a child to begin to imitate sounds and words. This can be very difficult for a young child with severe motor planning problems. If it doesn't ruin the song, help him perform the motions.

As with all of our play routines, eventually you want your child to sing songs with you for 10 minutes or longer.

Expand the Game:

1. Play the game with a new person. If this is a new game, you'll want to have the other person watch you first so they play it the same way that you do.

2. Try this game in a new place while you're waiting.

3. Fingerplays are a great distraction when you need to head off a meltdown or to redirect your child's attention when he's about to do something he shouldn't. I especially like this one since it gives your child something simple to do with his hands!

I CAN EVEN COUNT SOME MORE

<u>Materials</u>: None

<u>How to Play</u>:
This is a great extension for kids who love to count or who like to look at their fingers. Begin by holding up 2 fisted hands, and then chant,

One, two, three, four,
> (On one hand hold up index finger, middle finger, ring finger, and then pinky finger for each number as you count.)

I can even count some more.
> (Shake hand in a bouncing motion.)

Five, six, seven, eight.
> (On other hand hold up index finger, middle finger, ring finger, then pinky finger for each number as you count.)

All my fingers stand up straight.
> (Shake hand in a bouncing motion.)

Nine, ten are my thumb men.
> (Pop one thumb out on 9, then the next one on 10.)

Say the words slowly so your child can learn the words too, especially while counting.

After your child has watched you do this fingerplay for a couple of days, help your child begin to do the motions. Stop helping when he begins to hold up his fingers on his own.

Repeat this game a couple of times before moving on to a different activity. Remember, toddlers need lots of repetition to begin to recognize and then learn a new game.

Child's Goals:

The first goal is for your child to attend to what you're doing, stay with you, and watch your hand movements.

The primary goal of this song is for your child to join in counting.

Next we want her to try to imitate these simple hand motions by holding up her fingers (or trying). This is often difficult for a young child, especially those with motor planning problems, so accept any kind of motion that indicates she's trying to hold up her fingers. If it doesn't ruin the song, help her hold up her fingers.

As with all of our play routines, eventually your child should sing songs with you for 10 minutes or longer.

Expand the Game:

1. Play the game with a new person. If this is a new game, you'll want to have the other person watch you first so they play it the same way that you do.

2. Try this game in a new place while you're sitting and waiting.

3. Fingerplays are a great distraction when you need to head off a meltdown or to redirect your child's attention when he's about to do something he shouldn't.

WHERE IS THUMBKIN?

<u>Materials</u>: None

<u>How to Play:</u>
This is another great play routine for kids who like to look at their hands or fingers. Start with both fisted hands behind your back and sing,

Where is thumbkin?

Where is thumbkin?

Here I am.
> (Hold one thumb up and bend it several times as you bring it around to the front.)

Here I am.
> (Hold the other thumb up and bend it as you bring it around to the front.)

How are you today sir?
> (Wiggle your thumb as if it's "talking.")

Very well I thank you.
> (Wiggle your thumb as if it's "talking.")

Run and hide.
> (Return 1st thumb behind your back.)

Run and hide.
> (Return 2nd thumb behind your back.)

Repeat the next verses with your other fingers calling them:

Pointer, Middle, Ringer, Pinky

Here's the last verse:

Where's the whole family?

Where's the whole family?

Here we are.
>   (Bring first hand out wiggling all of your fingers as you bring them around to the front.)

Here we are.
>   (Bring other hand out and wiggle fingers.)

How are you today, sirs?
>   (Wiggle your fingers as if "talking.")

Very well we thank you.
>   (Wiggle your fingers as if "talking.")

Run and hide.
>   (Return 1st hand behind your back.)

Run and hide.
>   (Return 2nd hand behind your back.)

This is a long song! Be sure you're saying the words slowly so your child can learn the words too.

After your child has watched you do this fingerplay for a couple of days, help your child begin to do the motions. Stop helping when he begins to try to do the motions on his own.

Since this song is long, you may not be able to hold your child's attention to repeat it several times. But remember, toddlers need lots of repetition to begin to recognize and then learn a new song.

Child's Goals:
The first goal is for your child to attend to what you're doing, stay with you, and watch your hand movements.

The primary goal of this song is for your child to try to imitate these simple hand motions by holding up his fingers, or at least trying. This is often difficult for a young child, especially those with motor planning problems, so accept any kind of motion that indicates he's trying to hold up his fingers. If it doesn't ruin the song, help him hold up his fingers.

As with all of our play routines, eventually you want your child to sing songs with you for 10 minutes or longer.

5 LITTLE FINGERS

<u>Materials</u>: None

<u>How to Play</u>:
This is a great extension for kids who like to count or who love to look at their fingers. Begin by holding up one fisted hand, and then chant,

One little finger (Hold up index finger)

Says hello (Bend finger)

Where is my friend? (Twist finger)

What do you know! (Hold up next finger)

Two little fingers (Hold up two fingers)

Say hello (Bend fingers)

Where is our friend? (Twist fingers)

What do you know! (Hold up next finger)

Three little fingers (Hold up three fingers)

Say hello (Bend fingers)

Where is our friend? (Twist fingers)

What do you know! (Hold up next finger)

Four little fingers (Hold up four fingers)

Say hello (Bend fingers)

Where is our friend? (Twist fingers)

What do you know! (Hold up thumb)

Five little fingers (Hold up all 5 fingers)

Say hello (Bend fingers)

Here are our friends! (Twist fingers)

What do you know! (Shake hand)

Be sure you're saying the words slowly so your child can learn the words too.

After your child has watched you do this fingerplay for a couple of days, help your child begin to do the motions. Stop helping when he begins to try to do the motions on his own.

This is a long fingerplay! Repeat it a couple of times if your child likes the routine, but stop if you're losing him. Toddlers do need lots of repetition to begin to recognize and then learn a new game, but you may only get to do this one a couple of times before you need to move on to something new.

Child's Goals:

The first goal is for your child to attend to what you're doing, stay with you, and watch your hand movements.

Next we want her to try to imitate these simple hand motions by holding up her fingers, or at least trying. This is often difficult for a young child, especially those with motor planning problems, so accept any kind of motion that indicates she's trying to hold up her fingers. If it doesn't ruin the song, help her hold up her fingers.

As with all of our play routines, eventually your child should sing songs with you for 10 minutes or longer.

Expand the Game:

1. Play the game with a new person. If this is a new game, you'll want to have the other person watch you first so they play it the same way that you do.

2. Try this game in a new place while you're sitting and waiting. Alternate it with other "counting" fingerplays like the previous song, "I Can Even Count Some More."

3. Fingerplays can be a great distraction when you need to head off a meltdown or to redirect your child's attention when he's about to do something he shouldn't.

TWO LITTLE PUPPETS

<u>Materials</u>: None

<u>How to Play</u>:
This is another great game for kids who love to look at their hands. When your child is looking at his hands, hold yours where he can see them and chant,

Two little puppets,

> (Hold up both hands)

One on each hand,

> (Wave hands)

Isn't she pretty?

> (Look at your right hand and wave fingers)

Isn't he grand?

> (Look at left hand and wave fingers)

Her name is Bella,

> (Wave right fingers)

His name is Beau,

> (Wave left fingers)

Hear her say, "Good morning!"

> (Bend right hand)

Hear him say, "Hello!"

> (Bend left hand)

Be sure you're saying the words slowly so your child can learn the words too.

After your child has watched you do this fingerplay for a couple of days, help your child begin to do the motions. Stop helping when he begins to try to do the motions on his own.

Repeat this game a couple of times before moving on to a different activity. Remember, toddlers need lots of repetition to begin to recognize and then learn a new game.

Child's Goals:

The first goal is for your child to attend to what you're doing, stay with you, and watch your hand movements.

Next we want her to try to imitate these simple hand motions by holding up her hands (or trying). This is often difficult for a young child, especially those with motor planning problems, so accept any kind of motion that indicates she's trying to bend her hands. If it doesn't ruin the song, help her do the motions.

As with all of our play routines, eventually your child should sing songs with you for 10 minutes or longer.

Expand the Game:

1. Play the game with a new person. If this is a new fingerplay, you'll want to have the other person watch you first so they play it the same way that you do.

2. Try this game in a new place while you're sitting and waiting.

3. Fingerplays are a great distraction when you need to head off a meltdown or to redirect your child's attention when he's about to do something he shouldn't.

TEN LITTLE INDIANS

<u>Materials</u>: None

<u>How to Play</u>:
Hold up one finger at a time for each number you sing until you're holding up all 10:

One little, two little, three little Indians.

Four little, five little, six little Indians.

Seven little, eight little, nine little Indians.

Ten little Indian boys (or girls).

At the end, open your mouth and make an Indian noise by saying, "Aaaaaah," and patting your open hand against your lips.

This is an easy sound many toddlers will try to imitate. If he doesn't try the hand motion to his lips, place your hand there and model, "Aaaaaah," for him to imitate.

Repeat this game several times before moving on to a different activity. Remember, toddlers need lots of repetition to begin to recognize and then learn a new game.

<u>Child's Goals:</u>
The first goal is for your child to attend to what you're doing, stay with you, and watch your hand movements.

The primary goal of this song is for your child to say, "Aaaaaah," at the end and pat his own mouth.

Next we want him to try to imitate these simple hand motions by holding up his fingers (or trying). This is often difficult for a young child, especially those with motor planning problems, so accept any kind of motion that indicates he's trying to hold up his fingers. If it doesn't ruin the song, help him hold up his fingers.

As with all of our play routines, eventually you want your child to sings songs with you for 10 minutes or longer.

<u>Expand the Game:</u>
Sing with a new person and in new places.

RAIN, RAIN GO AWAY

<u>Materials</u>: None

<u>How to Play</u>:

Sing this song slowly when your child has noticed it's raining outside.

Rain, rain go away. Come again another day.
> (Hold both hands up and then move down wiggling your fingers like it's raining.)

Little children like to play.
> (Point to your child. If you sign with your child, sign the word for play by holding out your thumb and pinky fingers on both hands and wiggle.)

Rain, rain go away.
> (Hold both hands up and then move down wiggling your fingers like it's raining.)

Be sure you're saying the words slowly so your child can learn the words too.

After your child has watched you sing this song a couple of times, help your child begin to do the motions. Stop helping when he begins to try to do the motions on his own.

Repeat this song several times before moving on to a different activity. Remember, toddlers need lots of repetition to begin to recognize and then learn a new song.

<u>Child's Goals</u>:

The first goal is for your child to attend to what you're doing, stay with you, and watch your hand movements.

Next we want him to try to imitate these simple hand motions. If it doesn't ruin the song, help him perform the motions.

As with all of our play routines, eventually you want your child to sing songs with you for 10 minutes or longer.

<u>Expand the Game</u>:

1. Sing this song with a new person. If this is a new song, you'll want to have the other person watch you first so they sing it the same way that you do.

2. Try this song in a new place, especially when it's raining.

RAINDROPS

<u>Materials</u>: None

<u>How to Play</u>:

If all of the raindrops
>   (Wiggle fingers in the air.)

Were lemon drops and gum drops
>   (Tap one index finger on the palm of the other hand.)

Oh what a rain it would be.
>   (Hold both hands out to your sides.)

I'd stand outside with my mouth open wide
>   (Point to your chest on "I," and then point to your mouth on "mouth.")

Ah ah ah ah ah ah ah ah ah ah!
>   (Look up with mouth open saying, "Ah.")

Ah ah ah ah ah ah ah ah ah ah!
>   (Look up with mouth open saying, "Ah.")

If all of the snowflakes
>   (Wiggle fingers in the air.)

Were candy bars and milkshakes
>   (Tap one index finger on the palm of the other hand.)

Oh what a snow it would be.
>   (Hold both hands out to your sides.)

I'd stand outside with my mouth open wide
>   (Point to your chest on "I" and then your mouth on "mouth.")

Ah ah ah ah ah ah ah ah ah ah!
>   (Look up with mouth open saying, "Ah.")

Ah ah ah ah ah ah ah ah ah ah!
>   (Look up with mouth open saying, "Ah.")

During this song I always try to act silly on the "Ah ah ah" line to attract more attention, especially for children I've lost in all of those complicated words! Move your head and shoulders from side to side, bounce, or do silly motions with your arms if you've lost your child's attention.

Be sure you're singing the words slowly so your child can learn the words too. However, this song has LOTS of words that likely won't make sense to a language delayed toddler, and I've rarely seen a child on my caseload who can sing any word of this song other than the "Ah ah ah" part! This part is a real attention-getter, and I've seen several non-verbal children who rarely imitate anything try to say, "Ah ah ah," after I've sung this song several times.

Repeat at least the first verse several times before moving on to a different activity. Remember, toddlers need lots of repetition to begin to recognize and then learn a new song.

Child's Goals:

The first goal is for your child to attend to what you're singing, stay with you, and watch your hand movements.

The primary goal of this song is for your child to say, "Ah, ah, ah," at the end of the verse. If it doesn't ruin the song, help him perform the other motions, but the "Ah ah ah" part is really the primary piece I try to elicit from toddlers. I don't do the motions for the other parts of the song most of the time.

As with all of our play routines, eventually you want your child to sing songs with you for 10 minutes or longer.

Expand the Game:

1. Sing this song with a new person. Have them watch you first so they can sing it the same way you do.

2. Try this song in a new place. This is a great one to sing when it's raining or snowing outside.

3. Singing is a great distraction when you need to head off a meltdown or to redirect your child's attention when he's about to do something he shouldn't.

WHOOPS JOHNNY!

<u>Materials</u>: None

<u>How to Play</u>:

This is a game played by older children and teenagers. You can Google it to see the "trick" to the game. Young children won't understand the trick, but many toddlers and preschoolers LOVE this fingerplay because of the funny word and action for, "Whoops!"

Here are the words, followed by the actions.

Johnny, Johnny, Johnny, Johnny,

Whoops Johnny,

Whoops Johnny,

Johnny, Johnny, Johnny.

Hand motions - Hold up your left hand with fingers and thumb spread apart. Point your index finger on your right hand. Starting at the little finger, when you say each, "Johnny," touch the tip of each finger on the left hand with your index finger from the right hand. When you say, "Whoops," slide your right index finger down along the side of the left index finger and up the side of the thumb. For the next "Johnny," touch the tip of the left thumb. For the second, "Whoops," reverse the action of the first Whoops. The last four "Johnny's" reverse the actions of the first four. You should end up at the pinky finger of the left hand again.

It may also help to Google this game so that you see how to do these tricky motions, rather than read the directions!

Repeat this game several times before moving on to a different activity. Remember, toddlers need lots of repetition to begin to recognize and then learn a new game.

Child's Goals:

The first goal is for your child to attend to what you're doing, stay with you, and watch your hand movements.

The hand motions for this routine are probably too difficult for most toddlers, but many preschoolers will try and try!

The primary goal of this song is for your child to say, "Whoops!" After you've done this fingerplay for a while, pause and give him a chance to imitate this silly word. Pause and look expectantly at him just before you say, "Whoops!"

As with all of our play routines, eventually you want your child to sing songs with you for 10 minutes or longer.

Expand the Game:

1. Play the game with a new person. If this is a new fingerplay, you'll want to have the other person watch you first so they play it the same way that you do.

2. Instead of Johnny, you can say other family names to play this game. When you're playing and pointing to your child's fingers in this game, say his/her name. When you're playing with your fingers, use your name. This is a great way to work on Mama and Dada or even siblings' names.

3. If your child really likes this game, it's a fun one to use to redirect his attention. You may use this as a "warm up" for another activity when you need to get his attention first.

4. If your child begins to say, "Whoops," don't forget to use this word at other times.

SHE'LL BE COMIN' ROUND THE MOUNTAIN

<u>Materials</u>: None

<u>How to Play</u>:
This song has lots of words, so don't try to sing the whole thing unless your child loves it. Sing slowly so your child has time to process and keep up!

She'll be comin' round the mountain when she comes.

(Move both arms in a circular motion at your sides like a train's wheels moving.)

Woo! Woo!

(With one hand reach up and pull the train's whistle.)

She'll be comin' round the mountain when she comes.

(Repeat previous motions for these words.)

Woo! Woo!

(Repeat previous motions for these words.)

She'll be comin' round the mountain,

She'll be comin' round the mountain,

She'll be comin' round the mountain when she comes.

(Repeat same motions as before.)

Woo! Woo!

(With one hand reach up and pull the train's whistle.)

<u>Other verses:</u>

She'll be ridin' six white horses when she comes.

> (Hold one hand in front like you're holding a horses' reigns & pat the side of your leg with your other hand.)

Whoa back!

> (With both hands make a motion as if you're pulling back the horses' reigns.)

She'll be wearin' pink pajamas when she comes.

> (Start with hands at chest and then move hands down body as if showing off clothes.)

Scratch! Scratch!

> (Scratch chest.)

Oh, we'll all go out to meet her when she comes,

> (Move hands in front like running.)

Hi, Babe!

> (Wave hello.)

O, we'll eat chicken and dumplings when she comes.

> (Do the "eat" sign.)

Yum Yum!

> (Rub tummy.)

Oh, she'll have to sleep with grandpa when she comes.

> (Put palms of hands together and lay hands on head like sleeping.)

Snore, snore!

Even though this is an up-tempo song, be sure you're singing the words slowly so your child can keep up with you.

After your child has watched you do this song for a couple of days, help your child begin to do the motions. Stop helping when he begins to try to do the motions on his own. Again, this song is so fast that many children will happily listen without doing the hand motions, and that's okay!

Don't try to do this entire song unless your child loves it. Repeat a couple of verses several times before moving on to a different activity. Remember, toddlers need lots of repetition to begin to recognize and then learn a new game.

Child's Goals:

The first goal is for your child to attend to what you're doing, stay with you, and watch you. If a child is happily listening, I don't do the motions every time.

The primary goal of this song is for your child to stay with you and listen to you sing. He may also try to imitate the hand motions.

As with all of our play routines, eventually you want your child to be able to sing songs with you for 10 minutes or longer.

Expand the Game:

1. Sing this song with a new person. If this is a new song, you'll want to have the other person watch you first so they sing it the same way that you do.

2. Try this song in a new place.

3. If your child is playing with a train or horses, sing this song to help expand his play with a new idea.

4. Since this is such a fun and catchy song to hear, it's a great distraction for many children.

Solutions for Problems during Play

Sometimes, despite your best efforts, young children with language delays don't seem to want to play with you. This situation might look like a "behavior" problem, meaning that the child is purposefully *choosing* not to play *with* you. That's not always the case. Let me help you look at these problems from another perspective.

Nearly all "problems" we see during play could also be viewed as sensory processing differences. Most children who have difficulty interacting with others also have sensory processing issues. If this is a new term for you, please do some additional research to help you understand this diagnosis. Sources I suggest are listed in the Recommended Reading section. For the sake of clarity, I've included a brief explanation here.

Sensory processing disorder is the most current diagnosis for explaining differences in the way some children see, feel, smell, taste, hear, and understand the world around them. Their little bodies and brains literally don't sense these things the way other people do. Sometimes these incoming sensations are more intense than what others experience, and sometimes they are less intense. Because these children don't process these sights, sounds, smells, tastes, and how things feel like other kids do, their behaviors, both during play and during everyday routines, aren't what we would expect.

For example, activities you might find very ordinary and boring, like opening and closing a door or watching a ceiling fan, might be so visually exciting for your child that he wants to do it over and over again. Jumping off the cushions of a couch might seem like a dangerous activity for one child who is not quite sure if her body will cooperate, but for another child, jumping off the back of the couch ten times in a row isn't enough. Foods you consider to be "normal" in a kid's diet might be rejected by your child due to how it feels in his mouth or even how it smells. Your child might refuse to eat much of anything unless it's crunchy, or spicy, or very bland. Sounds that seem routine in every day life, such as the vacuum cleaner or a musical toy, might scare your child. However, this same child might not respond to his name, even when you're yelling for him.

If you feel that your child demonstrates many of these sensory processing differences, an occupational therapist who specializes in sensory processing disorders can evaluate your child, help you understand *why* your child is behaving the way he is, and determine overall treatment strategies that would be helpful. I highly recommend that you pursue this service if you need assistance in this area. You'll also find other resources listed in Chapter 6, Recommended Reading.

In this chapter you'll find practical ideas to help you address challenges that commonly arise during play with a child with social and communication delays. The key is to figure out a way to make play more enjoyable so that your toddler can participate. On each page you'll find:

- Problem
- Similar situations in What This Might Look Like
- Possible explanations for why your child is behaving this way
- Possible solutions for each challenge

If one suggestion doesn't seem to work for you or your child, try another one. Children with social and language delays with sensory processing differences can be puzzling, and usually it takes multiple attempts to find a solution for a problem during play. One idea you try may work beautifully one day, and the next day, or in the next 5 minutes, the same thing may not work at all. Let me encourage you to keep trying, keep exploring, and keep playing, despite all the hard work and energy it requires. One day you will see your efforts pay off!

PLACES TOYS IN MOUTH

What This Might Look Like:
Child puts toys in his mouth rather than playing with them

Possible Explanations:
1. Your child may be under-reactive to taste and craves more input in his mouth.

2. Oral exploration is your child's favorite way to process incoming information.

3. If your child is well over 2 and continues to put lots of toys in his mouth, he may also have a cognitive delay. He doesn't understand how to play with toys correctly yet, and he doesn't understand that he shouldn't put things in his mouth.

Ideas to Try:
1. Mouthing toys is developmentally appropriate until a child is near the age of 24 months old. For some children with delays, they may be well past their 2nd birthdays before they reach this maturity level. Until then, don't let him play with anything so small that he might choke on it unless you are fully focused on him.

2. Provide things that are more acceptable and safer for her to chew. Get a chewy tube or teething toy, and attach it to her shirt with a pacifier clip. When she starts to place a toy in her mouth, offer her the teether instead. Usually this works well, and she can move on to manipulate the toy with her hands since her oral sensory need is fulfilled.

3. When a child persists in mouthing or chewing a toy that's not safe, offer a crunchy or chewy snack instead. Try dried fruit, fruit snacks, pretzels, chips, string cheese, or cheese puffs/balls. This will satisfy his need to chew as you have a snack and play.

4. Show your child how to play with a simple toy over and over giving hand-over-hand assistance to help him learn what to do.

5. Use the bigger toys and movement games in the Early Toys section. She won't be as likely to want something in her mouth if she's up and moving.

6. If you've tried these other ideas, but you still feel there may be a behavioral component to continued mouthing, redirect your child. I say, "Yucky! Yucky!" as I remove the toy from a child's mouth. Then demonstrate how to use the toy appropriately as you say, "Don't eat the _____. That's yucky! Let's play! See?"

AVOIDS INTERACTION WITH PEOPLE

What This May Look Like:

Roams around or watches things rather than playing with people or toys

Lies on his back or tummy and turns away when you approach or talk to him

Seems bored or disinterested often

Seems to be "thinking" about something else when you talk to her

May be attached to parents and siblings, but doesn't interact with others

Doesn't respond to your attempts to get his attention or get him to talk

Looks past you when you're trying to get her attention or call her name

Possible Explanations:

1. Your child could be under-reactive to speech, which means he may not be aware you're talking to him. He isn't *choosing* to ignore you or tune you out. He's not processing that you're speaking to him and needs more stimulation to register that you're there and want his attention.

2. Your child could be over-reactive to environmental sensations. It's too noisy, the lights may be too bright, or the unpredictability of the events around her are making her shut down. She needs fewer distractions so that she can focus on you.

3. Your child likely has language comprehension delays and doesn't understand what you're saying to him. Even though he may be very smart in other ways, he's not consistently linking meaning to your words and phrases when you're trying to get him to play. Receptive language delays nearly always accompany social delays in toddlers. Because a young child regularly tunes out words, he doesn't understand them yet.

Ideas to Try:

1. Make your interactions with him much more playful. This doesn't necessarily mean louder, but use exaggerated facial expressions, simple words, and bigger actions that are energetic and FUN! He may need all of that extra input to know that you're talking to him. Otherwise, he doesn't recognize that your words are directed to him and that you <u>expect</u> him to respond to you. Pick a couple of Easiest Beginner Routines to start.

2. SING! Many children respond better to music than spoken words. Sing your child's name or another song she likes when you want to get her attention such as "Where Oh Where" from the Easiest Beginner Routines chapter. A sing-song, melodic way of speaking can also help a child become aware of you and respond to your voice. One more note - if your child covers his ears when you sing songs, it's usually not your

voice! He likely has auditory sensitivities. Try a different tone of voice singing higher or lower, sing softly, and always use fewer words.

3. Say a silly word like, "Yoo hoo," in a melodic way to grab her attention and lure her back to you when she's wandering away. Some children respond better to another new noise to alert their systems. Try clapping, whistling, an animal sound she likes, a fake cough or sneeze, or playful stomping toward her to begin a game.

4. Touch your child when you want his attention so he can feel you near him. Deep pressure is usually more calming and less aversive than light touch, so pick him up, give him bear hugs, rough-house, snuggle, squeeze, and tickle him to capture his attention.

5. Get in her line of vision to interrupt what she's looking at rather than you. Sit down on the floor with her. Do your best to put yourself face to face, even if that means you lie on your stomach to place your face in her space. If she's staring outside, get between her and the window. This also means moving fast to where she's going if she's moving away. Many children look at you more often when you're seated just below eye level, so put him up on a couch or low table, and you sit down on the floor to play.

6. If you've determined that he's shutting down when he's over-stimulated, modify those environmental factors. If there's too much noise in the room, turn off the TV or get away from the other kids to play. However, don't let his response be your excuse not to try to engage him. As I said in the introductory chapters, it's your job to help him learn to tolerate you, like being with you, and finally to respond to you so that he can learn to communicate. He's not going to learn to talk by being alone since interaction is the foundation for language development. Kids learn to talk from being with their parents and other people they love, not being isolated in their own little worlds, even if that seems like it's all he wants to do.

7. Begin with what your child already likes. This is what professionals mean by, "Follow a child's lead." Instead of showing her something new every time you want to interact with her, join in her play. If she's looking at her doll, cover the doll's eyes and say, "Where's baby? BOO!" If he's lining up cars, playfully place your hand over the next car, act surprised that it's gone, and call the car to come back. If he's on his back looking at his fingers, wiggle your fingers there too, and then begin your tickle game. If you lose her, try something different, but keep trying! For more information about these kinds of ideas, Dr. Stanley Greenspan has written extensively about this approach in his books. See the Recommended Reading section for more specific information.

DOESN'T LIKE TOYS

What This Might Look Like:
Roams around or watches things (including TV) rather than playing with toys
Seems bored or disinterested in most toys
Throws a toy rather than playing
Seems to be "thinking" about something else when you try to show him a toy
Pays more attention to the box or wrapping paper when she receives a present
Covers ears or acts scared of toys, particularly those that make noise
Likes one particular toy to the exclusion of everything else

Possible Explanations:
1. Your child could be under-reactive to the toy. This could mean the toy doesn't have enough "oomph" to interest her, or you're not being playful enough or showing her how to play. She isn't necessarily *choosing* to ignore you or tune you out. It doesn't always mean she doesn't like the toy; she doesn't like it yet!

2. Your child could be over-reactive to the sensory properties of the toy. Is there a big reaction, and he's getting up and moving away from the toy? Or is it more subtle? Is he turning away, leaning on you, closing his eyes, rubbing his face, or giving you other subtle cues that something about the toy may be a little too much for him?

3. Your child may have a motor planning problem which means he doesn't know how to play with the toy because he can't operate it on his own yet. Often times young children with motor planning problems can't open, close, push, pull, hook, catch, or even place their fingers in the right place to perform the correct actions to play with a toy. A child may pick up the toy and turn it over as if he's "checking it out" or "wondering how it works" rather than playing with it. Instead of learning what to do, he walks away and appears disinterested. Or he may become so frustrated that he throws the toy, rather than learning how to play with it the way he should. Remember, this is a situation when he *can't* play, not that he *won't* play.

4. Your child may have cognitive delays so that she doesn't know how to play with the toy. The toy may be too advanced for her, and she needs some help to learn to play.

Ideas to Try:
1. If your child is not interested in people either, start with the Easiest Beginner Routines to help him learn to interact first with you, then with toys.

2. Try ideas from the Early Toys section since all of these activities are easy and FUN! Sometimes the toys we're trying to introduce are too complicated. Try something else.

3. For a child who appears to tune out, try a toy with more movement and visual excitement, but with less buttons to push. Try bubbles, balloons, light up balls, or even toys that are a little more advanced, such as the games Fishing Around, Lucky Ducks, Elefun, the Fisher Price Super Spiral Speedway race track, or My Little Pony Ferris Wheel. These toys can be found at most major retailers such as Walmart or Target.

4. If a child overreacts consistently to a particular toy or a kind of toy, such as all things that make noise, put it away for a while until his system matures. Losing him during play isn't worth exposing him to a new toy he's not ready for yet. I often hold children in my lap when I think the toy may be over-stimulating for them, and this may help. Holding and reassuring usually helps form a stronger emotional bond with any child.

5. For a child with motor planning problems or a child with cognitive delays, repetition is vitally important while he is learning how to play. Show your child over and over how to play. Take his hand and place it on the right button, help him hook the trains, or put the car in the right place on the race track until he gets the hang of it. As soon as you see that he's beginning to do it himself, reduce your assistance. Start with one simple movement and practice that part many times before moving on to the next action. Praise his attempts. If you feel a meltdown coming on, or your child is about to throw the toy across the room because it's too hard to operate, gently reassure him, and happily provide help so that he stays with it, and you!

6. Let me also interject that some traditional activities are particularly difficult for kids with social, language, and sensory processing challenges. Although looking at books or trying to name flashcards may be important to you as a parent, since you feel like you're "teaching" your child new words, it's an activity that many toddlers don't enjoy. Sometimes a child might like to look at books, but only if he's in total control, and then he's likely tuning you out. If your child routinely takes the book from your hands, or becomes mad when you try to talk about the pictures, he's likely focused on getting visual feedback from the books. You might try changing the time of the day you use books, and instead of reading, label pictures. Books are often best at bedtime as part of your routine when your child is lulling down. Many education experts suggest making books available all day, but if your child doesn't let you look at and talk about the pictures with him using simple words and short phrases, he is not really learning language by reading books. Kids learn to understand words and name pictures while reading <u>with</u> someone else, not by looking at the pictures by themselves. During play time with you, opt for an activity that's more social and interactive if he's not ready yet.

LINES UP TOYS RATHER THAN PLAYING

What This Might Look Like:

Loves his Hot Wheels cars or Thomas Trains, but he doesn't really play with them
Repetitively spins the wheels so that he can watch them
Lines up or groups toys and gets mad if you mess up his order
Places toys in and out of a container rather than playing

Possible Explanations:

1. Your child may have such strong visual preferences that nothing else is as much fun for him as watching those wheels spin. He may like the visual pattern the cars make when he's lined them up bumper to bumper. He gets really mad when you disrupt his visual masterpiece since looking at this gives him more pleasurable feedback than anything else during play.

2. Your child may have motor planning problems which means he doesn't know how to play with the toy because he can't operate it on his own yet. Often times young children with motor planning problems can't open, close, push, pull, hook, catch, or even place their fingers in the right place to perform the correct actions to play with a toy. A child may prefer to line up the trains or spin a car's wheels since he can't do anything else yet. When you try to get him to do something else, he may become so frustrated that he protests or walks away, rather than learning what else he can do.

3. Your child may have an over-reactive sensory system and needs predictability and control, especially when he plays with his favorite toys. He may have such a low frustration tolerance level that he can't handle even the possibility that someone may try to mess up his order. He may not even like you there since he doesn't know what you'll do next.

4. Your child may have cognitive delays so that she doesn't instinctively know how to play with the toy, or the toy is beyond what she can figure out based on her previous experience. The toy may be too advanced for where she is right now, and she needs some help to learn how to play and use new ideas.

Ideas to Try:

1. Since you already know what your child likes, begin play with this toy. This is what professionals mean by, "Follow a child's lead." Instead of showing him something new, start with this toy that he already loves. If he's lining up cars, playfully place your hand

over the next car, act surprised that it's gone, and say, "Where's car?" Hide the car under his shirt or in his pocket, and then help him find it. Hide it in your shirt, behind your back, or under your leg. Put it under the cushion of the couch so you have to find it together. Drive it up your leg. Roll it off your arm or head. If he's on his back spinning the wheels, take another car and make it jump on top of the one he's holding saying, "Crash," or "Jump!" Stack the cars on top of each other to build a tower and say, "Boom" when they fall down. Do anything to get you included in his game! Even if he doesn't seem to like it at first, keep trying! Be sillier. Make the cars dance, or kiss, or sleep, or eat his toes. Make the car run over your fingers, which in turn, makes you pretend to cry. Sabotage what he likes to do, but in a fun way, so that he has to pay attention to you too. Even being a little irritated at you is a social response, so keep trying!

2. Expand play using one simple, related prop. If he likes trains, introduce a simple track so he can push the trains around. Find a station with doors so that he can place the trains inside and then take them out. For a child with motor planning problems, repetition is vitally important while he is learning how to play. Show your child over and over how to play. Take his hand and help him put the ball in the hole, or guide him to place the driver in the car, or fit the key in the door until he gets the hang of it. As soon as you see that he's beginning to do it himself, reduce your assistance. Practice that one new action many times in play before moving on to the next action. Praise his attempts. If you feel a meltdown coming on, or your child is about to throw the toy across the room because it's too hard to operate, gently reassure him, and happily provide help so that he stays with it, and you! When this step gets easier for him, introduce one more new action to expand this same play routine.

3. If he likes to line up or group a certain type of toy, introduce a similar toy to the mix. For example, if he likes trains, introduce small cars, trucks, or motorcycles to expand his interests and give you something new to talk about. If he likes to group small plastic Army men, introduce small plastic dinosaurs or zoo animals. If he has one particular container that he likes to store his Army men in, try a new container, and make them hop from bucket to bucket. Or turn the container upside down to make a "mountain" and have the Army men climb up and then jump off the top. When he likes that, add one more similar idea to expand this same play routine.

4. Don't use too many new words or talk too much while he's learning how to expand his play in this new way. Pick a few key words and short phrases and say them over and over to build language comprehension and add predictability to his play. Sometimes children leave play when we over-stimulate them with too much new language.

HOLDS TOY INSTEAD OF PLAYING

What This Might Look Like:
Holds a toy in one or both hands most of the time and doesn't want to let go
Seems like he's obsessed with one particular toy and refuses other things

Possible Explanations:
1. There's nearly always a sensory explanation for this behavior, rather than a true toy preference. Many kids like to hold things in one or both hands because of the tactile feedback, or sensations from touch, they receive. If you'll look at his hands, he's probably squeezing the item frequently because he craves this sensation. Some children hold an item because it stabilizes them. Clumsy and uncoordinated children may not know where their bodies are in space, but when they're holding a toy, they know exactly where their little hands are.

2. Some children do become attached to a toy because of other sensory feedback. If he's holding onto a video cover, he may like the picture or the glare from the cover as it hits the light. If he loves to hold trains, he may like to watch the wheels spin. If his preferred item is a blanket, rubbing the soft surface or the frayed ends may calm him.

3. A child who holds things rather than playing may also have difficulty motor planning. He doesn't play with many toys because he can't operate them on his own yet. Often times young children with motor planning problems can't open, close, push, pull, hook, catch or even place their fingers in the right place to perform the correct actions to play with a toy, but they *can* hold that object, so this is what they like to do! Some children don't insist on one particular toy, but gravitate toward a particular shape, like long and thin items such as a stick from a tree when they're outside, or a drumstick, marker, or spoon when inside. Instead of playing with something new, he walks away and appears disinterested. Remember, this is a situation when he *can't* play; it's not that he *won't* play.

Ideas to Try:
1. Be more fun with a new toy to entice him to play! A child will give up the item he's holding if he thinks he's getting something better. Show him how to play with another toy and act like you're having the time of your life so that he'll want to try too.

2. Incorporate his preferred item into your play. There were similar ideas in the previous section Lines Up Toys Rather Than Playing. If he likes to hold his bottle or

sippy cup even when it's empty, try to get him to give a doll, a stuffed animal, or you a drink. Hide the item he likes to hold under his shirt or in his pocket, and then help him find it. Hide it in your shirt, behind your back, or under your leg. Put it under the cushion of the couch so you have to find it together. Do anything to make that item part of the game so that you're "playing" with the item rather than letting him continue to hold it and do nothing else. Let me caution you that you have to be really, really fun and exciting when you do this, or else he's not going to understand that you're playing, and he may fall apart or shut down. I'd also suggest that you have a plan for what you are going to do with the object BEFORE you try to take it from him, or else he might think you're taking it just to be mean, and that will drive him away from you. This is not your goal, for this, or any other game you're attempting with him right now.

3. Offer a similarly sized item that will give him the same feedback during play. If he likes to hold his cars, try a small plastic animal or character. If he likes to hold a stick, try a spoon and have him "feed" a doll or stuffed animal. He still gets the sensation he likes, but you're expanding what he can do in play.

4. A child who holds things will often have difficulty using his hands in play. Try easy games with both hands so that he receives tactile feedback to his hands as he plays. Pop bubbles with a loud, hard smack to the floor with your open palm. Help him play games with vigorous hand clapping, and hold his hands a little more tightly during your games such as, "Row Your Boat," "Ring Around the Rosies," or "Ride a Little Horsie." Use other kinds of tactile play like play-doh so that you can show him how to roll, pound, and squeeze the play-doh so that he learns to use his hands for different things. Try the song Clap, Two, Three, Four on page 134 since this introduces lots of simple hand movements for him to copy. Place yogurt, pudding, or whipped cream on his high chair to play in and eat. Fill a medium to large plastic container with beans, pasta, sand, or rice, and then hide small toys in the mix so that he can dig to find them with both hands. If he doesn't want to touch the new material, give him a "tool" to use like a small, plastic shovel or spoon for digging, or you can offer a plastic knife, a rolling pin, or cookie cutters with play-doh. Try simple toys with tools too, such as a ball and hammer toy or a drum or xylophone with a stick for hitting to make music.

5. Keep showing him HOW to play with toys by offering hand-over-hand assistance. As soon as you see that he's beginning to do it himself, reduce your assistance.

REPEATEDLY PUSHES BUTTONS

What This Might Look Like:
Prefers electronic toys with lights and music to all other toys
"Gets stuck" pushing buttons over and over for long periods of time
Ignores other people while pushing buttons
May exhibit odd, or stereotypic, or other self-stimulatory behaviors such as flapping or leaning in for a closer look so that he gets extra visual feedback

Possible Explanations:
1. Your child has strong visual preferences or he is under-reactive to visual stimuli, so he craves toys that give him extra visual feedback, especially those with blinking lights.

2. Your child may have motor planning problems or low muscle tone. The only action he can consistently complete with a toy is pushing buttons.

3. Your child may have cognitive delays, so he prefers the simplicity of toys that can be activated with one push of a button. He may not understand how to play with more complex toys yet.

Ideas to Try:
1. In order to help your child move on to new activities, you may need to put these kinds of toys away. If there's another use for the toy, remove the batteries. If that's still not a viable option for you, at least limit the availability so that you give him the toy when you need a few minutes to take a shower or make a phone call. Remember, your child is not learning to communicate, connect with you, and relate to other people when he's stuck pushing buttons. Children learn to talk and understand words during real interactions with loving parents, not from an electronic toy, even if it's marketed as "educational." Don't get sucked into this false belief from toy manufacturers.

2.Try other toys that also provide visual feedback without the bells and whistles of the electronic toys. Many of the toys and activities listed in the Early Toys section have visual components such as bubbles and balloons. You can try other easy toys such as Lucky Ducks, Fishin' Around, or other games with parts that move to capture your child's attention, but that require more complex participation than repetitively pushing a button.

3. Children often get stuck in this kind of play because they don't interact with people very well or very often. Try games in the Easiest Beginner Routines section.

4. Show him how to play with a simple toy with hand-over-hand assistance to help him learn what to do. Read ideas from the two previous sections.

PREFERS TV/VIDEOS TO PEOPLE AND TOYS

What This Might Look Like:
Zones out when he's watching a video so that it's very hard to get his attention
Would watch TV all day if you let her
May be echolalic and quotes lines from a favorite show

Possible Explanations:
1. Your child has strong visual preferences. Or as surprising as it may sound, your child could even be under-reactive to visual stimuli, which is why he craves it so much.

2. Favorite TV shows and movies are very predictable, whereas real life is not. Your child knows what's coming next, and she prefers organization and routine to novelty.

3. Your child often feels over-stimulated and uses TV to "zone out" and block or recover from this uncomfortable feeling.

Ideas to Try:
1. For this kind of child who has difficulty interacting with others, TV and videos should be used only occasionally, and truth be told, not at all. He's not going to learn to interact with others if he's spending too much time in front of a screen. This goes for a DVD player in the car too. Save those movies for long cross-country trips when he's upset and you've tried everything else, not every time you get in the car for a trip to the grocery store or waiting in the carpool line everyday. Use that time to interact with him, especially since he's captive and still! Many of the Easiest Beginner Routines can be carried out in the car once your child has learned the routine at home. Or play a CD with music if you must, but know that real live singing, even with an off-key mom or dad, is better for your child than any professional musician!

2. Make your play with your child more fun and visually exciting. Be more animated! Use big facial expressions, gestures, and silly words to captivate his attention.

3. Capitalize on your child's interests. If your child likes one particular show, learn what songs, catch phrases, and "themes" the show uses, and carry those over to your play. Most current TV shows for kids market toys based on the characters. If your child loves to watch Dora, get a Dora doll and feed her, put her to bed, help her jump, and make her knock over a tower of blocks. If your child likes watching Elmo, sing the Elmo's World song he's heard many times as you play with an Elmo doll. Play your new games over and over since you know your child likes repetitiveness and things she can predict. Using what she already loves from her shows will expand her interest to you and toys.

SENSITIVE TO TOUCH

What This Might Look Like:

Doesn't hold or touch new textures in play

Resists holding your hands to walk in a parking lot or store

Plays by himself and becomes upset if you want him to join a group of peers

Doesn't like to be held

Refuses to wear certain clothes, may reject all new clothes, and fights diaper changes

Doesn't like to walk on grass or sand with bare feet

Walks on tip-toes (to avoid feeling his entire foot on the ground)

May not enjoy being tickled, but often this kind of touch is okay since it's deep pressure

Possible Explanations:

1. Your child has an over-reactive sense of touch, so he wants to avoid touching things that might make him feel uncomfortable. This is called "tactile defensiveness."

Ideas to Try:

1. Deep pressure is usually more acceptable to these children than light touch, so use a firm grasp when trying to hold her hand or change her clothes.

2. Try letting him have more control with touch, especially during play. Hold your hand out for him to grab, or slide your hand under his, or offer your finger instead. One of my friends who's an OT reminded me that holding a finger is actually a primitive reflex that some kids are still very comfortable doing, even when they don't like holding your hands. (Thank you Cindy Morgan!)

3. Don't force him to touch a new texture like play-doh, or even a new food, but make it available and show him how to touch it. Sometimes using a "tool" to touch the object first makes it easier. Use a roller or cutter with play-doh, and offer a utensil with new foods. If you're hiding items in a box of beans, pasta, sand, or rice, let him use a spoon or shovel to dig with before you encourage him to touch the offensive substance with his hands.

4. While some children with tactile sensitivities may initially reject vibrating toys and textured toys like a Koosh ball, they may begin to love them after repeated exposure. Don't force it on your child, but give him an opportunity to see you enjoying the new toy, and then let him try playing at his own pace.

5. If your child doesn't like being held, try sitting beside her, holding her on your lap further away from your body, or letting her lean on you. This isn't a rejection of you. Her system just can't handle that much direct touch without becoming over-stimulated.

6. Honor his clothing choices as much as you can right now. Many times this particular sensitivity gets better as a child matures and his system becomes more "normalized." Wear sandals at the beach, cut the tags out of clothes, and buy new clothes made from materials you know he likes and can tolerate.

7. Approach him from the front so that he can see you coming and knows you're going to touch him. If your child goes to preschool, you may want to have a discussion with the teacher about his sensitivities and give her some ideas for how to handle this at school. Peers are often so unpredictable during play and especially during times like forming a line. Perhaps your child could hold the door for the line or be in the back where he can tag along without "fear" and apprehension of being touched by surprise.

8. An occupational therapist (OT) can help you determine other solutions. The Wilbarger Deep Pressure and Proprioceptive Technique (DPPT), commonly referred to as the Brushing Program, is often recommended for children with tactile sensitivities. An OT can teach you how to properly administer this technique.

OTs also tell us to "prepare" a child's body before any activity they might not like, but especially for a touch that's unpleasant. Movement activities like running or jumping help our systems feel calmer and organized. Run a lap or two in your home or bounce your child on the couch or bed before changing his diaper or clothes or doing something in play he might not want to touch.

I frequently use this song as a way to "prepare" a child's body for something he might not like, especially holding my hands. Sing to the tune of "Here We Go Round the Mulberry Bush." Begin at a child's feet and work your way up his body for each verse gently squeezing each body part several times as you sing:

"This is the way we squeeze your feet, squeeze your feet, squeeze your feet.

This is the way we squeeze your feet, early in the morning."
> (Or "all day long" if you prefer this line to "early in the morning.")

Sing new verses as you squeeze his calves, thighs, shoulders, arms, and then, finally his hands. Skip squeezing your child's stomach or chest since this will make him more likely to vomit, urinate, or pass gas!

USES PARENT'S HAND TO OPERATE TOYS

What This Might Look Like:

Grabs an adult's hands to perform an action
Leads you to or puts your hand on items he wants
May not point or gesture very much on his own

Possible Explanations:

1. Your child likely has motor planning problems which means he doesn't know how to play with a toy because he can't operate it on his own yet. Often times young children with motor planning problems can't perform the correct actions to play with a toy. The child knows this on some level, but he also knows that your hands *can* do it! He has learned that his parents' hands can do things his can't, so he prefers to use yours.

2. Your child may be over-reactive to touch, so he wants to avoid touching things that might make him feel uncomfortable. This is called "tactile defensiveness." Read the previous section for an explanation and new ideas to try in play.

Ideas to Try:

1. Your child needs to learn to use his own body. Play simple games that help him learn to use his hands. Try simple games from the chapter Fingerplays and Songs such as Patty Cake, If You're Happy and You Know It, and So Big. Play other games like popping bubbles using two hands. Zip and unzip Ziploc bags. If your child can't operate simple cause and effect toys, start with this kind of play. I like the Fisher Price Super Spiral Speedway, simple pop up toys, and ball and hammer toys since a child can accomplish the goal for play with one or two simple actions.

2. Use hand-over-hand assistance to help him perform the action he wants you to do for him. Take his hand and show him how to complete the task. If he grabs your hands to clap or have you do signs, gently place your hands outside his and help him do most of the work. Gradually reduce your help so that you're touching him further down his arm or holding his elbows to guide him and not his hands. When he's trying to get you to do something, help him a little, and then let him do the rest. For example, if he wants you to open a top, unscrew it for him, but let him take it off.

3. See what will happen if you make your hands less available to him. Some children do reach and begin to point when you pretend you don't know what he wants. Hold your hands behind your back when he's trying to reach for them, but make it playful and fun so that he's not so frustrated that he can't try to complete the task on his own.

ODD, REPETITIVE, STEREOTYPIC, or SELF-STIMULATORY BEHAVIOR

What This Might Look Like:
Hand - flapping or twirling

Repetitive eye blinking

Moving fingers or his hands in front of his eyes

Rubbing skin or hair

Rocking back and forth or side to side

Smelling or licking objects or people (such as mom's hair)

Staring at lights or things that spin like fans or wheels

Possible Explanations:
1. Your child exhibits strong sensory preferences and craves the input he receives when performs this behavior. Or in some cases, he could even be under-reactive and need more of a particular input to register the sensory experience. For example, kids that stare at ceiling fans likely have strong visual preferences. A child who likes to smell things may have an under-reactive olfactory system and needs extra time or potent odors to essentially smell the item.

2. Your child could use his action, such as twisting his hands, as a way to rev up his sensory system, or it may occur involuntarily when he's excited. We often see kids flap their hands when they see something they really like. Other children might bite themselves or someone else when they are overly excited.

3. Your child could also use one of these behaviors as a way to calm down. If he's over-stimulated, he may rock, stare at the lights, rub his fingers together, or may twirl his mother's hair to calm down enough to go to sleep. This is a way to help block out the over-stimulating environment and refocus internally.

Ideas to Try:
1. Although a parent's first inclination is to tell your child to stop, helping him find a more acceptable way to get the result he's seeking is ultimately more successful in diminishing the behavior. For example, a child who likes to flap her hands might respond to clapping instead. A child who might hurt himself by biting can be given a chewy tube to bite. If a child likes to spin objects, try to use toys that are designed to spin, instead of spinning things that aren't. If a child likes to rock, get a rocking chair.

2. If your child really seems to be stuck in a behavior, like rocking or spinning, try to make it more communicative so that he includes you. Use the rocking games in the Easiest Beginner Routines. Grab her hands and dance slowly and rhythmically with her.

THROWS TOYS

What This Might Look Like:

Throws toys instead of playing

Possible Explanations:

1. Your child may have a motor planning problem which means he doesn't know how to play with the toy because he can't operate it on his own yet. Often times young children with motor planning problems can't open, close, push, pull, hook, catch, or even place their fingers in the right place to perform the correct actions to play with a toy. The child knows this on some level, becomes frustrated, or doesn't want to try, so he throws the toy instead.

2. Your child may be over-reactive to touch, so he wants to avoid touching things that might make him feel uncomfortable. This is called "tactile defensiveness." Read the ideas in the section Sensitive to Touch on page 166.

3. Your child may have language comprehension delays and does not understand, "No throwing!" Even though he may be very smart in other ways, he's not consistently linking meaning to your words and phrases when you're telling him how not to play.

4. Your child may have cognitive delays so that she doesn't instinctively know how to play with the toy, or the toy you're using is beyond what she can figure out based on her previous experience. The toy may be too advanced for where she is right now and that is frustrating for her. She throws the toy rather than playing.

5. Your child may have low muscle tone and have difficulty manipulating objects. Throwing may be one thing he can consistently do. If your child is picking up and releasing the object beside or behind him and seems to be unaware of this, as opposed to launching the toy across the room and then looking to see where it is, he's likely dropping the item rather than throwing.

6. Your child may not want to play anymore, but she doesn't know to transition in an acceptable way. However, if she's throwing often, look for one of the other reasons as the root cause.

Ideas to Try:

1. If your child is not interested in people either, start with the Easiest Beginner Routines to help him learn to interact first with you, then with toys.

2. You may be trying a toy that's too difficult. Simplify your activity. Try to play with ideas from the Early Toys section since all of these activities are easy and FUN! Sometimes the toys we're trying to introduce are too complicated. Parents are surprised when I suggest that we try something that's simpler when a child walks away and appears to be bored.

3. For a child with motor planning problems or for a child with cognitive delays, repetition is vitally important while he is learning how to play. Show your child over and over how to play. Take his hand and place it on the right button, or help him hook the tractor's trailer on, or place the farmer in the tractor to drive, or open the barn door until he gets the hang of it. As soon as you see that he's beginning to do it himself, reduce your assistance. Start with one simple movement and practice that part many times before moving on to the next action. Praise his attempts. If you feel a meltdown coming on, or your child is about to throw the toy across the room because it's too hard to operate, gently reassure him, and happily provide help so that he stays with it, and you!

4. For a child who repeatedly throws, be sure you consistently say, "No throwing!" and shake your head for no, so that he begins to understand that you don't like it when he throws his toys, food, or anything else for that matter. For some children, making them pick up the object does seem to lessen how often they do this. Hold your child's hand and make him walk over to pick up the item, and then take it back to where you were seated. Don't make this part of your play fun, or your child will see this as an extension of the game. I change my voice and facial expression so that a child gets the message that I am not happy when he throws over and over again. If your child really seems to be finished with the activity, begin your clean up routine.

5. Your child may also be throwing to get a reaction from you. If you've made it a fun part of your routine, you may want to rethink this! If your child is seated in a high chair, the thrill of dropping the item all the way to the floor and then watching you retrieve the object is sometimes more fun than playing. In this case, sit with him on the floor to play since it won't be nearly as exciting as watching a toy fall from the high chair.

6. If your child is not acting upset, looking for the item he threw, or watching for your reaction, he's likely not "throwing" the toy on purpose. In this case, you'll need to work to increase his strength in his upper body, arms, hands, or fingers. An occupational or physical therapist can evaluate your child and help you determine how to work on overall strength and motor skills.

CONSTANT MOTION

What This Might Look Like:
Child can't sit still and likes to run, jump, spin, and crash
Has no fear and may not cry when he gets hurt
Has a very short attention span
Plays with one toy for a few seconds then moves on to something else
Needs constant supervision since she'll get hurt or break something
Doesn't understand your rules or listen when you tell him "no" or "stop"
May walk on his toes (to feel even more pressure in his toes)

Possible Explanations:
1. Your child is likely a "sensory seeker." He may be under-reactive to movement and constantly needs MORE action to feel it through his little body.

2. Some children move more when they are over-stimulated. They don't know how to calm down, or self-regulate, on their own. He may have to work himself into a frenzy and then "crash" before he's able to stop moving.

3. Your child may also have a language comprehension delay and doesn't understand your words or rules when you're telling him to stop or slow down. He may have to hear your loud voice or see your angry facial expressions to realize that he's in trouble.

Ideas to Try:
1. Instead of trying to fight his need to move, embrace it. Adjust your rules and expectations knowing that sometimes your child can't help it – he's got to go! Give him more opportunities to run, jump, spin, and crash throughout the day. Get outside more often. It's okay to let him jump on the bed with supervision, or run back and forth from one end of your house to the other. Many times a young child's behavior improves significantly when he gets 20 to 30 minutes of movement every 3 hours or so. An Occupational Therapist can help you come up with creative ways to address a child's need to move.

2. Build movement into play *with* you. Try the Easiest Beginner Routines with running, chasing, tickling, swinging, and jumping. Use ideas from the Early Toys section that involve movement in the game such as throwing and chasing balls, popping bubbles, and catching balloons. Make roughhousing, wrestling, or tackling a game you play several times a day, and not just with Daddy!

3. Try sit down play activities AFTER he's had an opportunity to move around for a while. When he does need to sit to play, bounce him gently on your lap. All play with this kind of kid has to be even more energetic, even when you're sitting down. Increase your energy level with your voice so that you're more animated and fun, even if you're doing a puzzle or playing with blocks.

4. Sometimes children leave play when it's too complicated and go on to find something they do understand. Make your play and your words very simple and repetitive, especially if your child doesn't understand many words. Look for ideas in the Early Toys section. Use games from Chapter 2, Easiest Beginning Social Routines or the simple fingerplays and songs in Chapter 4.

5. If you feel your child getting over-stimulated, offer a cold drink from a straw and/or a crunchy or chewy snack. Sucking and chewing are often very regulating for children who have a hard time calming down.

6. For some children with balance issues or significant sensory processing challenges, using a boundary to mark off their play space is important and can help curb the need to move. The boundaries help them recognize where their bodies are in space, and they are more focused when they are sitting to play. The most obvious and practical solution for this kind of child is to use a high chair or another seating system. In therapy sessions, I use the high chair as a last resort when I've provided several different movement activities, and they haven't been successful to help a child regulate and calm down. Other kinds of seating alternatives I like to try are a bean bag or a child-sized chair for the child to sit in while I sit in front of them on the floor. I've also used a rug or blanket placed on the floor so a child could "see" our play area. If he tries to run away, say, "Come back here. This is where we play." When I ran a language playgroup program, I used carpet squares for circle time so that a child had a movement "job" at the beginning and end of the activity by retrieving and then putting away his carpet square, and he had the benefit of a visual boundary to see where he needed to sit and stay during circle time.

7. If your child is constantly in trouble because he's so busy, adjust your expectations, and modify your environment so that you don't have to police your home as often. Set aside a large area that's safe for play by removing all breakables and other things you're afraid might hurt him. If you have the room, consider purchasing a swing for inside, a smaller inflatable ball pit, or a toddler-sized trampoline with a bar so he can bounce without tearing up your furniture. Read <u>Sensational Kids</u> by Lucy Miller or <u>The Out of Sync Child Has Fun</u> by Carol Kronowitz for more ideas.

SHORT ATTENTION SPAN

What This Might Look Like:
Quickly moves from one toy or activity to the next
Can't sit still to complete an activity

Possible Explanations:
1. Your child may be a "sensory seeker." She may be under-reactive to movement and constantly needs MORE movement to feel it through her little body, so she can't sit still for very long.

2. Some children move more when they are over-stimulated. They don't know how to calm down, or self-regulate, on their own. He may have to work himself into a frenzy or even have a meltdown before he's able to stop moving.

3. Your child may also have a language comprehension delay and doesn't understand your words or rules when you're playing. He may need to try to move on to find something that's meaningful or more fun for him.

Ideas to Try:
1. If you feel your child has a short attention span because he's a sensory seeker and needs more movement, then you'll need to give him more opportunities to move throughout the day. Try the ideas from the previous section Constant Motion.

2. Try sit down play activities AFTER she's had an opportunity to move. When she does need to sit to play, bounce her gently on your lap. Play with this kind of kid has to be even more energetic, even when you're sitting down. Increase your energy level with your voice so that you're more animated and fun, even if you're playing with a doll house.

3. Try to extend your play "one more turn" by having him complete one more, small step during your activity. For example, if you're playing with Potato Heads, have him place one more piece on Mr. Potato Head. If you've been playing with a ball and hammer toy, have him place the ball in the hole and hit it "one more time."

4. Add a clean up routine to all play activities since this automatically extends the time she spends with each activity. Insist that she help you clean up before she moves on to

the next toy. If you've seen my DVDs, you know that I put all of my toys in giant 2 ½ gallon Ziploc bags. Unzipping the bag is the first step we do in play. Putting the items back into the bag and zipping the bag closed are the last steps we do for every single activity, every single day. Say the same phrase and sing the same "Clean Up Song" each time you clean up such as, "All done. Let's clean up." The song and phrase teach your child that cleaning up is part of play.

If he tries to run away before this is done, get up and chase him down, and then take him back to the toys to clean up. If your child is balking about picking up all of the Legos or each piece of the train track, help him do it, especially in the beginning. For some children who have never done this before, picking up even 1 or 2 pieces and putting them away before running to the next activity is a very big deal, so celebrate the smallest successes. Clap and cheer for your child each time he's put a piece away. Gradually increase the number of items he has to put in the bag so that eventually you're holding the bag, and he's doing most of the work. There are numerous examples of my clean up routines in each of my DVDs, so take a look at those if you need more help with this.

5. Sometimes children leave play when it's too complicated or when you've over-stimulated him with too many new words. Make your play and your words simple and repetitive, especially if your child doesn't understand much yet.

6. If you feel your child is getting over-stimulated, offer a cold drink from a straw and a crunchy or chewy snack. Sucking and chewing are often very regulating for children who have a hard time calming down.

7. For some children, using a boundary to mark off their play space is important and can help curb the need to move. The boundaries help them recognize where their bodies are in space, and they are more focused when they are sitting to play. The most obvious and practical solution for this kind of child is to use a high chair or another seating system. In therapy sessions, I use the high chair as a last resort when I've provided several different movement activities, and they haven't been successful to help a child regulate and calm down. Other kinds of seating alternatives I like to try are a bean bag or a child-sized chair for the child to sit in while I sit in front of them on the floor. I've also used a rug or blanket placed on the floor so a child could "see" our play area. If he tries to run away, say, "Come back here. This is where we play." When I directed a language playgroup program, I used carpet squares for circle time so that a child had a movement job at the beginning and end of the activity by retrieving and then putting away his carpet square, and he had the benefit of a visual boundary to see where he needed to sit and stay during circle time.

AGGRESSIVE

What This Might Look Like:
Child bites, hits, scratches, kicks, or lunges at you or another person

Possible Explanations:
1. Your child may be over-stimulated. Many children jump on you or even bite you when they are overly excited. They're not being mean on purpose, but they don't know how to control their emotions and impulses.

2. Toddlers and young children do become aggressive when they are genuinely mad. This seems to happen more often with a child with language delays since he doesn't yet have the words to tell you what he wants, express disappointment, or explain how he feels.

Ideas to Try:
1. Watch for signs of over-stimulation and gradually help your child calm down. Abruptly stopping the activity isn't recommended because the child could then have a meltdown which might prompt aggression. If you've been jumping, running, and having a great time, but sense that your child is about to "go over the edge," grab his hands and begin to slowly bring his excitement level down with a rhythmic song and dance or a bounce on your lap.

2. Some kids tackle or push you because they enjoy this play and crave the deep pressure they feel from pushing you. Or they like being tackled and assume you do too! If you don't like to play this way, or if your child is big enough to hurt you, try to provide the same kind of input for him in a more acceptable way. Bounce him harder during a game of "Ride a Little Horsie," or find a safe way for him to run, jump, and crash. Try building a mountain of pillows or cushions from the couch and let him jump and tackle away!

3. If your child is aggressive because he's mad, you can't let him hurt you, someone else, or even himself. If you feel this building, try distraction well before he reaches his boiling point and hurts someone. Move on to something else when you see his frustration escalating. He'll have plenty of opportunities to learn to "work through it" since there will be those situations when you can't avoid a full-blown meltdown. Prevent the ones you can!

4. If he does continue to become aggressive, the easiest thing to do is remove yourself from his reach so that he can't hurt you. Stand up and move a little farther away from him while speaking in a firm, yet loving tone. Completely leaving the room he's in isn't recommended either. Isolating a child with social and interactive problems is not the way to discipline him, even for aggressive behavior. We want a child to learn to love being with you, so placing him alone in his room for an extended period of time, or leaving him alone while you exit the scene, even for an adult-imposed "time out," is counter-productive for this type of child. I like to put children up on a couch where I can sit on the floor below them. They can still see me, but I can lean back and get out of harm's way if necessary, or grab him if he's about to hurt himself.

5. If a child is hurting himself, try a big bear hug from behind or hold him in your arms and begin swinging him to provide calming, deep pressure. If this makes your child too mad, put him down and step away until he calms down.

6. If your child is hurting another child, remove your child from the situation, but stay with him using your same loving, but firm tone and a brief explanation such as, "No hitting. Hitting hurts." Often times we stop and take care of the other child leaving the aggressor to get even madder since he has no one to help him calm down and regulate. While some professionals would recommend that you take care of the child who is hurt and "ignore" the child who has been aggressive, this can upset the aggressive child even more. When you're in a situation and someone else can tend to the child who's been hurt, remove your child, and help him calm down. He still needs to know you're mad and that what he's done is wrong, but you're there, helping him learn from his mistake.

TANTRUMS and MELTDOWNS

What This Might Look Like:

Becomes mad and screams, cries, throws himself on the floor, kicks, bangs his head, becomes aggressive with you, or hurts himself

Possible Explanations:

1. Many toddlers, even those without developmental delays, have tantrums and meltdowns. Sometimes these events seem to "come out of the blue," but most of the time, you can identify the triggers and signs before a full-blown episode occurs.

2. All young children (and adults too!) are more prone to lose their tempers when a physical need is unmet. If your child is thirsty, hungry, tired, gets hurt, has a wet/dirty diaper, or is sick, she is more likely to have a meltdown.

3. Some children have a very low frustration tolerance level. The least bit of difficulty can set them off. These children often have a meltdown when what you're doing is too challenging. Remember that your child feels helpless. In this case your child is not being manipulative, but truly needs your assistance to calm down.

4. Some children have meltdowns when they are over-stimulated. It may be too noisy, too bright, too windy, too hot, too cold, too *anything*, and it upsets their systems.

Ideas to Try:

1. I love what Dr. Stanley Greenspan says about meltdowns. His advice is to assume that your child does not hear you, understand you, and is out of control during a tantrum because... he is! This means no teaching can occur until you help him calm down. Many parents and therapists try to "push through" and use this moment saying, "He's got to learn!" The truth is, most children, and especially those with developmental issues, do not learn anything when they are that upset. Period. Children learn when they are calm, not in the middle of a meltdown. Do your best to help him regulate and get back to baseline so that he can begin to hear you and understand you. This means that you have to remain calm in the midst of the meltdown. Only one of you is allowed to be out of control, and it's not the adult!

2. First and foremost, promptly address any physical needs. Feed her a snack if it's been a while since she's eaten. Change her diaper if she's dirty. Put her down for a nap if she's sleepy. Children with developmental delays are often more at risk to "fall apart"

when their physical systems are compromised by even a little illness, fatigue, or hunger.

3. Help your child calm down. If you know there's not a physical need to be met, move on to what you know helps your child regain control. Is rocking or swinging comforting to her? Does she enjoy snuggling or being softly bounced on your lap? Does he respond to your gentle voice or stroking his hair? Does he need his blanket or sippy cup?

4. All young children do best with predictable routines. If your child is consistently having a meltdown during a particular play activity or with a daily routine, then you need to change what you're doing. That doesn't mean don't ever wash his hair, but find a way to do it that's less upsetting. An occupational therapist can often help you determine solutions for these kinds of problems with sensory processing components.

5. Redirection is best when you feel your child might possibly be headed for a meltdown. Show him something new or begin a different activity to divert his attention away from what's frustrating him or is about to get him in trouble! This also minimizes the chance he'll reach the full meltdown phase. Again, some parents and therapists feel that heading off every tantrum doesn't give a child an opportunity to learn, but remember that children with developmental social and language delays aren't going to learn much of anything in the middle of a meltdown, so if you can avoid it, give it your best shot. There will be plenty that you can't avoid, no matter what you try!

6. Simplify the activity if he's getting too stressed out. If the toy is too difficult for him to operate, do it for him, and then show him how to do it or guide his hands to complete the task. If he's getting upset about a particular toy, you may have to put it away and move on to something else. If he's mad that he's expected to share a toy, use two of the same toys so that he has one to hold while he's learning how to play. More advice for teaching sharing is listed in on page 183.

7. Avoid lengthy explanations or lecturing when your child is having a meltdown. Keep your words "short and sweet." Remain firm, but loving, giving brief directions and offering redirection when you can. "No candy. How about some grapes?"

8. One other successful thing I do when a child is about to lose control is to drop my voice to almost a whisper, hold a child's hands gently, and pull him in very close to my face to get his attention. This is usually such a stark contrast from how he's been handled in the past that it's an attention-getter. It usually helps by providing a big distraction (Me!), and serves to DE-escalate the moment by bringing the activity level down to a quieter, calmer place.

DIFFICULTY WITH TRANSITIONS

What This Might Look Like:
Gets mad when you want him to leave a place or put away a preferred toy
Becomes upset when you move from one daily routine to the next
Difficulty entering a new place

Possible Explanations:
1. Many toddlers, even those without developmental delays, and especially those with social and interaction challenges, have difficulty with transitions, or moving from activity to activity during play, or when they begin and end daily routines. Getting your child to come indoors from playing outside, settle down to sleep, get out of the tub, put away a toy, or turn off the TV can be difficult.

2. Many children with developmental delays and sensory processing issues are not flexible. They have difficulty moving on, particularly when it's not his or her idea.

Ideas to Try:
1. Keep your language very simple during transitions so that your child isn't lost in your words and doesn't understand what's coming next. Use key words and short phrases. Sometimes a picture schedule of the day's events can help a child understand transitions throughout the day. For more information about setting up picture schedules, read the related articles on my website.

2. Develop a transition routine in play. Give advance warning that you're almost ready to move on such as, "One more minute/time, then we're all done." Some experts recommend using a timer that rings to signal the activity is almost over, but this isn't always practical for parents, but may be a good idea for activities that are especially challenging for your child to stop. Say, "When we hear the beep, trains are all done."

3. Use the First/Then strategy, and offer the next activity. "First we clean up, then we _____." If your child routinely has meltdowns with a particularly difficult transition, try coming up with a pleasant "then" for the next activity. Offering a choice for the next activity gives a child a sense of control even when he's going to be upset. For example, when leaving the playground, ask, "Do you want to walk, or should Mommy pick you up?"

4. Predictable routines and songs can often help a child understand what comes next. Songs can help a child who wants to move on too quickly to slow down. These songs

and routines can also help a child who has difficulty moving on to the next event. Listed below are several songs I teach families to incorporate into their daily routines to make those transitions a little easier to handle.

CLEAN UP ROUTINE

Anytime you're cleaning up toys or an activity you've done together, picking up a mess in your home, or even doing the dishes after a meal, begin your clean up routine by singing the same "Clean Up Song." You can sing one you make up yourself, or search the internet until you find one you like. I sing Barney's "Clean Up, Clean Up" many times a day in therapy with my little friends. Here are the words:

"Clean up, clean up, everybody, everywhere.

Clean up, clean up, everybody do your share."

Many children start to hum or try to sing this song when they are ready to be finished with an activity. Watch carefully as your child begins to act like he's ready to move on, and sing the song yourself so that he can begin to sing too.

BATH TIME, MEALS, GETTING DRESSED, etc...

For daily routines such as eating lunch or taking a bath, I sing, "Do You Know What Time It Is?" Sing to the tune of, "Do You Know the Muffin Man?"

**"Do you know what time it is? What time it is? What time it is?
Do you know what time it is? It's <u>snack time.</u>"**

You could also try singing this one to the tune of "The Farmer in the Dell."

**"It's time to <u>brush your teeth,</u>
It's time to <u>brush your teeth,</u>
We've had some fun and played today,
It's time to <u>brush your teeth.</u>"**

Fill in the blank with whatever daily activity you're starting next.

Or try, "This is the way we _____," sung to the tune of "Here We Go Round the Mulberry Bush."

**"This is the way we put on socks, put on socks, put on socks.
This is the way we put on socks, early in the morning."**

You can sing:

Put on shoes/coat, change your diaper, go inside, take a bath, wash your face, wash your hands, dry your hands, wash the table, eat our lunch, etc....

GOOD BYE ROUTINES

Many children have difficulty leaving a favorite place or a person. Sometimes singing the "Bye bye Song" makes this easier. Wave and sing,

"Bye bye _____,

Bye bye _____,

Bye bye _____,

It's time to say good-bye."

Fill in the name of the person or even a place or object like, "Home," "McDonalds" or "Swings." Many children begin to say, "Bye bye," after you've been singing this song for a while.

If a child is having a rough time with mom or dad leaving, a good-bye routine can ease the transition. Develop something that's your special ritual. I kissed the back of my daughter's hand leaving a lipstick print there under her chubby little fingers. I'd tell her that I'd be back before my "kissy" was gone. Some moms blow 3 kisses for "I love you" and then make a quick departure. Dads can give hugs, high 5's, or fist bumps. Sometimes making a big deal out of mom or dad leaving can make the transition worse, so use your own judgment. I don't like to depart in secret, but sometimes it's the only way to avoid a huge meltdown when your child might happily play and not be too bothered by your absence if you've not made leaving such a big deal.

DOESN'T LIKE TO SHARE OR TAKE TURNS

What This Might Look Like:
Becomes mad and aggressive with you or another child during play with a toy

Possible Explanations:
1. Many toddlers, even those without developmental delays, have difficulty with sharing.

2. Many children with developmental delays and sensory processing issues are not flexible and aren't yet mature enough to share.

Ideas to Try:
1. If your child routinely has difficulty with sharing, look at your expectations during play. Typically developing children, those without a developmental delay, aren't cognitively mature enough to share until they approach 2 ½. This means that until your child is understanding and talking like a 2 ½ year old (following multiple step directions and using mostly 3 word phrases when he talks), he's not developmentally ready to learn how to share. Minimize how often he has to share his toys until he reaches that developmental level.

2. As a parent you can work on helping your child learn to share using the following method as described in Barbara Sher's book Early Intervention Games. This works best when you aren't using his favorite prized possession, but a toy he likes. Let your child play with the toy for a while as you sit next to him. Gently place your hand on your child's hand and say, "My turn." Help him let go of the toy. Hold the toy for just a second and then hand it back saying, "My turn," as a model for your child to eventually imitate. Repeat this sequence several times a day over the next few days. As the game is continued over the next few weeks, slowly increase the amount of time you hold the toy until you are briefly playing with the toy yourself. Over time he will learn that he always get the toy back and will begin to tolerate sharing and turn-taking with you. Once he's tolerating sharing with you, introduce sharing with another trusted adult such as dad or a grandparent. Learning to share with other children may take a while.

LOST IN OWN WORDS INSTEAD OF PLAYING OR LISTENING

What This Might Look Like:
Child may quote lines from a movie, song, or show
Child is talking to herself using words you don't understand

Possible Explanations:
1. Your child may be echolalic. Echolalia is frequently present in children who go on to be diagnosed with autism spectrum disorder. Echolalia is repeating or "echoing" what a another person has said. Children who are echolalic imitate what they have heard someone say in everyday life, lines from a book or song, or a script from a TV show or movie. Professionals most often characterize children as "echolalic" when many of the words or phrases a child uses seem to be repetitions from a previous activity rather than new utterances she comes up with on her own to convey meaning. Children with echolalia use "more advanced language" when they are repeating lines than they can typically generate on their own. For example, a toddler who is exhibiting echolalia can quote long segments from a favorite TV show or sing an entire song word for word, yet he can't ask for milk when he needs it, or answer a question his dad asks him. Even though this child "talks" since he can technically say lots of words, he doesn't seem to completely understand what he's saying. In essence, he's just repeating words without really being able to "use" them.

2. Your child may be using jargon, or unintelligible sentence-length utterances. Many parents describe this as "jibber jabber." Jargon is part of typical language development around the 18-21 month level when a child is trying to move from words to phrases and lacks the vocabulary to do this. In an older child, jargon frequently means that there are receptive language problems. He is trying to talk, but he doesn't understand words well enough to put them together in a way that can be understood. You may be able to pick out a real word or two, but the rest is "jargon."

3. Your child may be using sounds in a self-stimulatory way. A child may use a sequence of sounds like, "Diga diga diga," when she is excited. An older verbal child may repeat real words, phrases, or sentences to help calm down.

4. Your child may *possibly* be using real words with so many consonant and vowel sound substitutions that you don't recognize the word. Listen carefully to determine if this is the case. If he's using the same sequence of sounds for one particular item each

time he sees it, it may be his version of the word. Let me issue a word of caution here. Many parents believe a child is saying real words when there's no evidence that the child understands much of anything he or she hears. If your child is not following simple verbal directions and seems to tune you out much of the time, the "talking" he's doing right now is jargon. Hang in there though! Children have to be noisy before they can talk!

Ideas to Try:

1. For a child who seem to be stuck in her own words with jargon or echolalic utterances rather than tuning in to you, use ideas from the previous section Avoids Interaction on page 156 to work on helping her engage and interact with you.

2. For a child who is using a word or phrase in a self-stimulatory way when she's excited, model something she could say, such as, "Yay!" If she's using the word or phrase to help calm or regulate, try modeling a phrase which might fit the situation better such as, "I need help," or "I'm mad."

3. For a child who seems to be trying to communicate with you saying echolalic sentences that don't quite fit the situation, echolalia can give you an opportunity to know exactly what he or she is having difficulty learning. Echolalia can serve a purpose. For example, the child who is walking around aimlessly quoting a movie or book may need help in finding an appropriate activity, or he may be feeling stressed or anxious and uses this routine to calm himself. A child who asks his mother, "Do you want a cookie?" needs help in learning to initiate requests in a more appropriate way. A child who repeats a question needs help learning the meaning of the words so he can accurately process the question, or he may need specific cues to learn exactly how to answer. A child who repeats, "Good job (his own name)" needs to learn a declarative phrase such as, "I did it!" A child who repeats his brother's words may just be trying to take a turn in conversation and doesn't know what else to say. Other tips for working with a child with echolalia can be found on my website at teachmetotalk.com.

One more word about echolalia... Echolalia is a very positive indicator that your child is going to learn to talk. Let me remind you again of the bright side of echolalia. He's talking! She's trying! He *is* learning to communicate. You can see it right before your very own eyes! It may be frustrating for you right now, even for a long time, but remember that it's better than the alternative of your child remaining silent and not showing any evidence of learning language. The positive qualities of echolalia, a child's strong memory skills and a preference for predictable patterns, CAN and SHOULD be used to help your child learn to communicate. Use these suggestions and ask your SLP to help you figure out how best to do this for your child.

4. If you're in doubt if your child is using a real word, ask your child's speech-language pathologist what she (or he) thinks. Sometimes we have to reinforce a syllable your child uses before it really becomes a purposeful word, so keep trying!

REFERENCES and
RECOMMENDED READING

Greenspan, S. I., & Wieder, S. (2006). *Engaging autism*. Cambridge, MA: Da Capo Press.

Greenspan, S.I., & Lewis, D. (2005). *The affect-based language curriculum*. Bethesda, MD: Interdisciplinary Council on Developmental and Learning Disorders.

Greenspan, S. I., & Wieder, S. (1998). *The child with special needs: encouraging intellectual and emotional growth*. Washington, D.C.: Perseus Books.

Kranowitz, C. (2006). *The out-of-sync child*. NY, NY: Perigree.

LeComer, L., & Kranowitz, C. (2006). *The out-of-sync child has fun*. NY, NY: Perigee.

MacDonald, J. (2004). *Communicating partners*. Philadelphia, PA: Jessica Kingsley Publishers.

Marshalla, P. (2001). *Becoming verbal with childhood apraxia*. Millcreek, WA: Marshalla Speech and Language. www.pammarshalla.com.

Manolson, A. (1992). *It takes two to talk*. Canada: The Hanen Centre.

Miller, L., & Fuller, D. (2007). *Sensational kids*. NY, NY: Perigee.

Sher, B. (2009). *Early intervention games*. San Francisco, CA: Jossey-Bass.

Sonders, S. (2003). *Giggle time*. London, England: Jessica Kingsley Publishers.

Stamm, J., & Spencer, P. (2007). *Bright from the start*. NY, NY: Gotham Books.

Sussman, F. (1999). *More than words*. Canada: The Hanen Centre.

Swigert, N. (2004). *The early intervention kit*. East Moline, IL: LinguiSystems, Inc.

White, B. (1995). *The new first three years of life*. NY, NY: Fireside.